Briefcase on European Community Law

Second Edition

Susan Wolf, BA, LLB
Senior Lecturer in Law
University of Northumbria

Second edition first published in Great Britain 1999 by Cavendish Publishing Limited, The Glass House, Wharton Street, London, WC1X 9PX, United Kingdom

Telephone: +44 (0) 20 7278 8000   Facsimile: +44 (0) 20 7278 8080

E-mail: info@cavendishpublishing.com

Visit our Home Page on http://www.cavendishpublishing.com

Wolf, Susan 1959–

Briefcase on European community law – 2nd edn

1 European Union   2 Law – European Union countries

I Title

341.2'422

ISBN 1 85941 258 0

Printed and bound in Great Britain

Preface

The most significant development since the publication of the first edition of *Briefcase on European Community Law* in 1996 is, without doubt, the entry into force of the Treaty of Amsterdam. The Treaty of Amsterdam makes a number of substantive amendments to the EC Treaty and the Treaty on European Union; however, the renumbering of the Treaty Articles is likely to be the thing which causes the most confusion for students of EC law. Clearly, the case law and secondary legislation which pre-dates the Treaty of Amsterdam renumbering will refer to the 'old' Treaty numbers, whereas future legislation and cases will refer to the new numbers. The approach taken in this second edition is to refer, in the first instance, to the new Treaty numbers, as students will almost certainly be taught EC law by reference to the Treaty as it now is. However, the old Treaty number has also been included in parenthesis (for example, Article 28 EC (ex 30)). The area likely to cause the greatest confusion is in relation to the free movement of goods, where Article 30 has been renumbered as Article 28, and Article 36 has been renumbered as Article 30! Students are advised to take care when dealing with these particular changes. The only exception to this approach is in relation to quotations which refer to the former Treaty number. In addition, this book also includes a Table of Equivalences (see p iv), which sets out the pre- and post-Amsterdam numbering of the main Treaty Articles referred to in this book.

In addition to the obvious changes brought about by the Treaty of Amsterdam, the new edition includes a number of new important cases, for example, in the area of sex discrimination and the freedom of establishment.

Sincere thanks are due to my colleagues, Tony Storey with whom I share the majority of my EC law teaching and Elizabeth Griffiths for help and advice. Thanks also to Cara Annett at Cavendish Publishing, for her support in the production of this second edition.

Susan Wolf
August 1999

Abbreviations

AC	Appeal Cases
All ER	All England Law Reports
CA	Court of Appeal
CFI	Court of First Instance
Ch	Chancery Reports
CMLR	Common Market Law Reports
EAT	Employment Appeal Tribunal
EC	European Community
ECJ	European Court of Justice
ECR	European Court Reports
ECSC	European Coal and Steel Community
EEC	European Economic Community
EP	European Parliament
EU	European Union
Euratom	European Atomic Energy Community
HL	House of Lords
NHS	National Health Service
IRLR	Industrial Relations Law Reports
SDA	Sex Discrimination Act
SEA	Single European Act
TEU	Treaty on European Union
WLR	Weekly Law Reports

Contents

Table of Cases: Alphabetical

Table of Cases: Numerical

Table of Cases: UK Courts

Table of Legislation: European Treaties

Table of Legislation: European Secondary Legislation

Table of Legislation: UK Legislation

Table of Equivalences

European Community Treaty 1957

Previous numbering	New numbering
Article 2	Article 2
Article 3	Article 3
Article 3a	Article 4
Article 3b	Article 5
Article 3c	Article 6
Article 5	Article 10
Article 6	Article 12
Article 9	Article 23
Article 12	Article 25
Article 13 (repealed)	–
Article 14 (repealed)	–
Article 15 (repealed)	–
Article 16 (repealed	–
Article 17 (repealed)	–
Article 30	Article 28
Article 31 (repealed)	–
Article 32 (repealed)	–
Article 33 (repealed)	–
Article 34	Article 29
Article 35 (repealed)	–
Article 36	Article 30
Article 37	Article 31
Article 48	Article 39
Article 49	Article 40
Article 50	Article 41
Article 51	Article 42
Article 52	Article 43
Article 53 (repealed)	–
Article 54	Article 44
Article 55	Article 45
Article 56	Article 46
Article 57	Article 47
Article 58	Article 48
Article 59	Article 49
Article 60	Article 50
Article 61	Article 51
Article 62 (repealed)	–

Article 63	Article 52
Article 64	Article 53
Article 65	Article 54
Article 66	Article 55
Article 73m	Article 65
Article 73n	Article 66
Article 73o	Article 67
Article 73p	Article 68
Article 73q	Article 69
Article 85	Article 81
Article 86	Article 82
Article 95	Article 90
Article 96	Article 91
Article 100	Article 94
Article 100a	Article 95
Article 119	Article 141
Article 130r	Article 174
Article 130s	Article 175
Article 130t	Article 176
Article 145	Article 202
Article 146	Article 203
Article 147	Article 204
Article 164	Article 220
Article 165	Article 221
Article 166	Article 222
Article 167	Article 223
Article 168	Article 224
Article 168a	Article 225
Article 169	Article 226
Article 170	Article 227
Article 171	Article 228
Article 172	Article 229
Article 173	Article 230
Article 174	Article 231
Article 175	Article 232
Article 176	Article 233
Article 177	Article 234
Article 178	Article 235
Article 179	Article 236
Article 183	Article 240
Article 184	Article 241
Article 189	Article 249
Article 189a	Article 250
Article 189b	Article 251
Article 189c	Article 252
Article 190	Article 253
Article 191	Article 254
Article 235	Article 308

1 The Institutions of the European Union

1.1 The European Parliament

1.1.1 The Parliament's role in the legislative process

Roquette Frères SA v Council Case 138/79
The Council adopted a Regulation, under Article 37 EC (ex 43) of the EC Treaty, without having received the Parliament's opinion which the Council had requested. The Regulation was challenged by RF under Article 230 EC (ex 173) (see Chapter 4), on the grounds that there had been an infringement of an essential procedural requirement.

Held The ECJ held that the compulsory consultation of the Parliament as provided for by the EEC Treaty is the means by which the Parliament plays an actual part in the legislative process of the Community and, as such, represents an essential factor in the institutional checks and balances intended by the Treaty. Therefore, consultation of the Parliament required by the Treaty constitutes an essential procedural requirement. Any legal provision adopted without the opinion of the Parliament, where such an opinion is required, is null and void. The Council has to take all reasonable steps to obtain the Parliament's opinion.

European Parliament v Council Case C-65/90
When the proposal before the Council changes substantively, a fresh consultation of the Parliament is required.

1.1.2 The Parliament's right to bring judicial review proceedings

European Parliament v Council (Re Comitology) Case 302/87
This case concerned the position of the European Parliament in judicial review proceedings. Article 230 EC (ex 173) of the Treaty does not give the Parliament the privileged status granted to the Council and the Commission. Here, the Parliament sought to establish that it had privileged status, particularly since parliamentary acts were amenable to review. (See *Parti Ecologiste Les Verts v European Parliament*, below.)

Held The ECJ held that the Parliament was neither a natural or legal person nor did it have privileged applicant status. The Parliament had no right to bring an action for annulment. (Although see Advocate General Darmon's opinion that the Parliament should have been granted limited *locus standi* to defend its own prerogatives.)

European Parliament v Council (Re Chernobyl) Case C-70/88

This case followed the *European Parliament v Council (Re Comitology)* Case 302/87 above. The Parliament once again sought to establish its right to bring judicial review proceedings and sought annulment of Council Regulation 3954/87/Euratom. The Council had adopted this Regulation (following the disaster at the Chernobyl nuclear plant) under Article 31 of the Euratom Treaty by virtue of which the Council only had to consult Parliament. The Parliament argued that the Regulation should have been adopted under Article 100a (now 95 EC) of the EEC Treaty, which would have required adoption under the co-operation procedure (and, hence, a greater role for the Parliament).

Held In this case, the ECJ held that the Parliament has the right to bring an action for annulment providing that the action seeks only to safeguard its prerogatives and providing the action is founded only on submissions alleging their infringement.

Note ───
This judicial decision is now reflected in the Treaty as amended by the Treaty of European Union 1992. See Article 230 EC (ex 173).
──

European Parliament v Council (Re Transport Policy) Case 13/83

The Parliament brought an action under Article 232 EC (ex 175) on the grounds that the Council had failed to implement a Community transport policy, as required by Article 70 EC (ex 74). Also, that the Council had failed to adopt certain measures proposed by the Commission to achieve the freedom to provide transport services throughout the Community as required under Articles 49–51 and 71 EC (ex 59–61 and 75).

Held The ECJ held that the Parliament has the right to bring an action for failure to act under Article 232 EC (ex 175). It also held that the Council did have an obligation to bring forward measures relating to the free movement of transport services, but the action in relation to the general transport policy failed. The Court held that the requirement to develop a policy was not sufficiently precise to be enforced.

1.1.3   Actions of the Parliament are subject to judicial review

Parti Ecologiste Les Verts v European Parliament Case 294/83

The French Ecology Party sought the annulment of a decision taken by the Parliamentary Bureau to award funding to a number of groups ostensibly to fund an information campaign prior to the parliamentary elections. The provisions of Article 173 (now 230 EC) under the Treaty of Rome (prior to amendment by the Single European Act 1986) did not refer to acts of the Parliament as reviewable acts.

Held The ECJ held that Article 173 (now 230 EC) permitted the review of any measure of a Community instrument that could have binding effect. An interpretation of Article 173 (now 230 EC) which excluded measures adopted by the European Parliament from challenge would lead to a result contrary to the spirit of the Treaty. Consequently, measures adopted by the Parliament intended to have legal effect vis à vis third parties can be subject to an action for annulment.

Note ────────────────────────────────────
The EC Treaty now makes it clear that acts adopted jointly by the European Parliament and the Council are subject to review. See Article 230 EC (ex 173).
──

1.1.4   The Parliament has a right to intervene in cases before the Court of Justice

Roquette Frères SA v Council Case 138/79

For facts, see above, 1.1.1.

Held The ECJ also held that the Parliament has the same right as the Council and the Commission to intervene in any case before the ECJ. This right to intervene is granted by Article 37 of the Statute of the Court of Justice.

1.1.5   Direct elections to the European Parliament

Liberal Democrat Party v Parliament Case C-41/92

The Liberal Democrat Party in the UK brought an action under Article 232 (ex 175) of the EC Treaty, challenging the European Parliament's failure to draw up proposals for uniform procedures for the direct elections of its members as required under the Treaty. However, the action was struck out by the ECJ when the Parliament adopted a resolution on a uniform electoral procedure after the commencement of the legal proceedings.

1.2   The Commission of the European Communities

1.2.1   The Commission has complete discretion in Article 226 EC (ex 169) proceedings

Star Fruit Company v Commission Case 247/87
The Star Fruit Company brought an action under Article 232 EC (ex 175) in order to try to force the Commission to commence proceedings (under Article 226 EC (ex 169)) against France. The company alleged that, as a result of quotas on imports of bananas into France, it had suffered loss and had complained to the Commission and had asked the Commission to take action against France.

Held The ECJ held that the Commission is not bound to investigate or follow through all complaints nor is it bound to commence Article 226 (ex 169) proceedings. In fact, the Commission exercises discretion at all stages.

1.2.2   The Commission's right to take Decisions

Germany, France, Netherlands, Denmark and United Kingdom v Commission Cases 281, 283–85 and 287/85
This case was brought by the five Member States who sought the annulment of Commission Decision 85/381. The Decision related to the Community's immigration policy. The Member States argued that the Commission had exceeded its legal competence because the Treaty did not empower the Commission to adopt a binding decision in a field which fell within the exclusive jurisdiction of the Member States.

Held The ECJ held that where the Treaty confers a specific task on the Commission it must be accepted, if the provision is not to be rendered wholly ineffective, that it also confers on the Commission the power to carry out that task.

1.2.3   The Commission has the power to enter into international agreements

Commission v Council (ERTA) Case 22/70
In this case, the Member States, acting through the Council of Ministers, had resolved to co-ordinate their approaches in negotiations leading up to the European Road Transport Agreement (ERTA). The Commission challenged this resolution, arguing, *inter alia*, that the Commission had a right to participate in the conclusion of international agreements, and that it had, in fact, replaced the Member States as the competent actor in this field.

Held The ECJ held that in addition to express provisions in the Treaty (such as Articles 113 and 114 (now 133 EC) regarding agreements on tariff and trade) the Treaty implies that the Commission has the power to enter into international agreements.

1.3   The Council of the European Union

See *Roquette Frères SA v Council* Case 138/79, above, 1.1.1 and 1.1.4.

1.4   The law making powers of the institutions

1.4.1   The correct legal base

Commission v Council Case (Re Titanium Dioxide) Case 300/89

In 1989, the European Commission brought an action against the Council of Ministers arguing that the Council had incorrectly used Article 130s (now 175 EC) for the adoption of the Titanium Dioxide Directive (89/428/EEC). When the Commission originally proposed the Directive, it had put it forward as an internal market harmonisation measure under Article 100a (now 95 EC). However, the Council of Ministers subsequently decided (unanimously) to alter the legal bases and adopt the Directive under Article 130s (now 175 EC).

Held The ECJ decided in favour of the Commission. The Court held that, where there are two aims and therefore two possible legal bases, then normally both should be used. However, in this instance it was not possible to use both Articles 100a and 130 (now 95 and 175 EC) since the legislative procedures required under both were different. The Court came to the conclusion that the correct basis was Article 100a (now 95 EC). In reaching this decision, the court referred to the second paragraph of Article 130r (now 174 EC) which states that 'environmental protection requirements shall be a component of the Community's other policies'. They took this to mean that Article 130r–t (now 174–76 EC) was not the only provision of the Treaty concerned with environmental protection.

European Parliament v Council (Re Students' Residence Directive) Case C-295/90

The European Parliament challenged the Council's adoption of the Student's Residence Directive (90/36/EEC). The Council had adopted the Regulation under Article 235 (now 308 EC) which required the consultation of Parliament. However, Parliament argued that the Directive should have been adopted under Article 12 EC (ex 6) which required the co-operation procedure.

Held The ECJ held that the Directive had been based on an incorrect legal basis. The Directive was annulled.

Commission v Council Case 45/86

The Commission challenged a Council Regulation under Article 230 EC (ex 173) of the Treaty. The basis of the challenge was that the Council had not stated a precise legal base for the Regulation, contrary to Article 253 EC (ex 190), and that consequently the Council did not use the procedure under Article 133 EC (ex 113). The Commission contended that Article 113 was the correct legal base, but the Council adopted the Regulation using the unanimous voting procedure under Article 308 EC (ex 235).

Held It follows from the wording of Article 308 EC (ex 235) that its use as a legal base for a measure is justified where no other provision of the Treaty gives the Community institutions the necessary power to adopt the measure in question. The ECJ held that the Council had the power to adopt the contested regulations under Article 133 EC (ex 113) of the Treaty and the use of Article 308 EC (ex 235) was not justified.

European Parliament v EU Council (Re Trans-European Telematic Networks) Case C-22/96

In 1993, the Commission submitted a communication to the European Parliament suggesting two legislative proposals based on Article 235 (now 308 EC). After the entry into force of the TEU, the Commission substituted Article 129d (now 156 EC) which required the use of the co-operation procedure. The Commission then sought to replace the legal base back to Article 235 (now 308 EC), which only gave the Parliament the right to be consulted. The Commission in fact adopted Decision 95/468, using Article 235 (now 308 EC) and the Parliament sought annulment of this Decision.

Held The ECJ held in judicial review proceedings that the use of Article 235 (now 308 EC) as a legal base for a measure was justified only where no other Community provision gave the institutions the necessary power to adopt the measure in question.

1.5 The European Court of Justice

R v Henn and Darby Case 34/79

The UK banned the import of pornographic materials. Similar material in the UK was illegal if it was likely to 'deprave or corrupt', but imports were prohibited if they were 'indecent or obscene'. H and D were charged with illegally importing pornographic materials into the UK from Rotterdam. The case was referred to the ECJ under the preliminary rulings procedure (see Article 234 EC (ex 177)).

In his judgment, Lord Diplock said of the ECJ:

The European Court of Justice, in contrast to English courts, applies teleological rather than historical methods to the interpretation of the Treaties and other Community legislation. It seeks to give effect to what it conceives to be the spirit rather than the letter of the Treaties and other Community legislation; sometimes indeed, to an English judge, it may seem to the exclusion of the letter.

Note —————————————————————————————

The jurisdiction of the European Court of Justice is considered more fully in Chapters 3, 4 and 5.

2 Community Legislation

2.1 The EC Treaties – a new legal order

Costa (Flamino) v ENEL Case 6/64

C sought a declaration from the Italian court that he was not obliged to pay his electricity bill (less than £2!) on the grounds that the Italian law which had nationalised the electricity industry in 1962 and which had created the new company, ENEL, was contrary to certain provisions of the EEC Treaty including Article 31 EC (ex 37). The Italian court sought a preliminary ruling on the relevant Community law provisions. However, the Italian Government intervened once the matter was referred to the ECJ and argued that the application for a preliminary ruling was wholly inadmissible because the dispute involved matters of national law unconnected with the Treaty.

Held The EEC Treaty had created a new legal order which was an integral element of the legal systems of the Member States. By creating a Community of unlimited duration, with its own institutions, there had been a transfer of power from the Member States to the Community and the Member States had limited their sovereign rights.

It was held that the Italian court was under an obligation to apply Community law over a subsequent unilateral act incompatible with the Treaty. Consequently, Article 234 EC (ex 177) is to be applied regardless of any domestic law, whenever questions relating to the interpretation of the Treaty arise.

2.1.1 The EC Treaty has extra-territorial effect

Béguelin Import Co v SAGL Import-Export Co Case 22/71

B, a Belgian company, entered into an exclusive distribution agreement with a Japanese company, which gave B the exclusive right to distribute Japanese cigarette lighters in France. A similar distribution agreement gave exclusive distribution rights to a German company in Germany. SAGL, a competing French company, purchased the lighters in Germany, imported them into France and then attempted to resell them in France. B brought an action in the French Courts against SAGL to prevent them from selling the lighters in France. SAGL argued in return that the exclusive distribution agreement with the Japanese company was in breach of

Article 81 EC (ex 85) and was, therefore, void. The French Court sought a preliminary ruling asking the ECJ whether the provisions of the Treaty applied to agreements made with parties outside the Community.

Held The fact that one of the parties to an agreement is situated in a third country does not prevent the application of Article 81 EC (ex 85), since that party is operative within the Community. The Court extended the application of the Treaty, giving it extra-territorial effect.

2.2 Regulations

2.2.1 Regulations are directly applicable

Commission v Italy (Slaughtered Cow II) Case 39/72
The Commission brought proceedings against Italy, alleging that Italy had not applied the provisions of a number of Council Regulations concerning premiums for the slaughtering of cows.
   Held:

> According to the terms of Articles 189 and 191 [now 249 and 254 EC] of the Treaty, Regulations are, as such, directly applicable in all Member States and come into force solely by virtue of their publication in the Official Journal of the European Communities, as from the date specified ...

Consequently, all methods of implementation of Regulations are contrary to the Treaty because this could lead to a distortion of Community law throughout the Member States.

Leonesio v Ministero dell'Agricoltura e delle Foreste Case 93/71
Held Member States cannot subject Regulations to any national implementing measures, unless specifically required by the Regulation itself.

Fratelli Variola SpA v Amministrazione Italiana delle Finanze Case 34/73
A preliminary ruling was sought as to whether the provisions of a Regulation could be implemented by domestic measures which effectively reproduced the provisions of the Regulation.
   Held The direct application of a Regulation means that its entry into force in a Member State is independent of any national measure and that Member States are under a duty not to obstruct the direct applicability inherent in Regulations.

Commission v UK (Re Tachographs) Case 128/78
Council Regulation EEC/1463/70 made it compulsory to fit tachographs (mechanical recording equipment) on certain vehicles. The UK enacted a statutory instrument in order to implement the provisions of the EC

Regulation. The statutory instrument introduced a voluntary scheme for the introduction of the tachographs.

Held The ECJ held that, in Article 226 EC (ex 169) proceedings, Community Regulations are directly applicable, binding in their entirety, and cannot be applied by Member States in an incomplete or selective manner.

2.2.2 Regulations have general application

Zuckerfabrik Watenstedt GmbH v Council Case 6/68
This case involved a challenge by Z to a Council Regulation. The Regulation terminated price maintenance for producers of raw sugar beet with effect from a prescribed date. It affected less than 30 producers. The ECJ had to consider whether or not the measure, classified as a Regulation, was really a Decision in substance.

Held A Regulation is applicable to 'objectively determined situations and involves legal consequences for categories of persons viewed in a general and abstract manner'.

2.3 Directives

2.3.1 Implementation must be binding and effective

Commission v Ireland (Re Animal Semen Directive) Case C-236/91
Article 226 EC (ex 169) proceedings against Ireland for failure to implement Directive 87/328/EEC by the deadline of 1 January 1989. Ireland argued that whilst it had not adopted the required implementing legislation, it did observe the Directive in practice.

Held Ireland had not fulfilled its obligations under the Treaty. Implementation of a Directive must be legally certain, and cannot be fulfilled by mere administrative practices which by their nature are alterable.

Commission v Italy Case 168/85
In this case, the Italian Government argued that a Government Circular was sufficient to define the rights of nationals seeking to establish themselves in Italy, under the provisions of a Directive.

Held The ECJ held that mere administrative practices which by their nature are alterable by the authorities and which are not given the appropriate publicity cannot be regarded as proper fulfilment of a Member State's obligations under the Treaty. A Member State cannot rely on a circular to implement Community law.

Commission v Belgium Case 239/85

The Belgian Government issued a circular pending the amendment to its national rules needed to implement a Directive on waste (78/319/EEC).

Held In Article 226 EC (ex 169) proceedings against Belgium it was held by the ECJ that each Member State must implement Directives in a manner which fully meets the requirements of legal certainty and must consequently transpose their terms into national law as binding provisions.

2.3.2   Implementation must be effective

Von Colson and Kamann v Land Nordrhein-Westfalen Case 14/83

Von Colson was rejected when she applied to work in the prison service. She brought an action in the German courts on the grounds that the rejection was based on sex. The German court found in her favour but limited the award of damages to travelling expenses to and from the interviews. Von Colson argued that these damages contravened the Equal Treatment Directive (76/207/EEC) which requires Member States to enable persons claiming a breach of the equality principle to pursue their claims through the judicial process.

Held The ECJ held that:

> Member States are required to adopt measures which are sufficiently effective to achieve the objective of the Directive and to ensure that those measures may in fact be relied upon before the national courts

For a further discussion of this case, see Chapter 8.

2.4   Decisions, Opinions and Recommendations

Compagnie des Forges de Châtillon v High Authority Case 54/65

Here, the applicant sought annulment of a Decision addressed to itself. The ECJ defined a Decision as 'a measure emanating from the competent authority, intended to produce legal effects'.

Grimaldi v Fonds des Maladies Professionnelles Case C-322/88

A Belgian tribunal sought a preliminary ruling of a Recommendation.

Held National courts must take into account relevant recommendations and opinions when considering cases; particularly in circumstances where the recommendations help to clarify the interpretation of other national measures adopted in order to implement them, or where the recommendation supplements EC secondary legislation.

2.5   Article 249 EC (ex 189) is not exhaustive

Commission v Council (ERTA) Case 22/70

Discussions of the Council of Ministers concerning the attitude to be
adopted by the (six) Member States at the negotiations of the European
Road Transport Agreement (ERTA) were challenged by the Commission.
The Commission alleged that the Council proceedings amounted to an
encroachment by the Council on the Commission's area of responsibility.
The Commission brought an action to annul the proceedings. The Council
argued that the proceedings in question did not constitute an 'act' within
the meaning of Article 230 EC (ex 173).

Held The proceedings in question were designed to lay down a course
of action binding on both the institutions and the Member States and
accordingly had legal effect and as such were amenable to judicial review.
It would be wrong to restrict reviewable acts to those mentioned in Article
249 EC (ex 189).

2.6   The classification of acts is not conclusive

Confédération Nationale des Producteurs de Fruits et Légumes v Council Cases 16 and 17/62

A French association of fruit and vegetable producers brought an action
for annulment of a Regulation. Article 230 EC (ex 173) of the Treaty states
that natural and legal persons can only seek judicial review of decisions,
or Regulations which, although in the form of Regulations, are really
Decisions.

Held The ECJ held that it is the object and content of the measure that
is the determining factor, not the official title given to the measure. A
Regulation, being essentially of a legislative nature, is applicable to
categories of persons viewed abstractly and in their entirety. Here, the
Regulation in question failed to lay down general rules and was held to be
a disguised Decision.

Note ————————————————————————————————————

The classification of acts is important in judicial review proceedings – see
Chapter 4.

International Fruit Co NV v Commission (No 1) Cases 41–44/70

International Fruit brought a judicial review action before the ECJ,
challenging the validity of Council Regulation (EEC) 983/70. Under the
terms of Article 230 EC (ex 173), an individual or company can only
challenge a Decision or Regulation which is really a Decision.

Held Here, the Court found that Article 1 of the contested Regulation was not a provision of general application. The Court determined that the Regulation was really a conglomeration of individual Decisions. This illustrates how the ECJ will examine the substance of the measure rather than its official classification.

2.7   Article 253 EC (ex 190) – duty to state reasons

Germany v Commission (Re Brennwein) Case 24/62

The German Government challenged a Commission Decision which granted Germany a wine tariff quota below the level requested by the Member State.

Held The ECJ held that, in order to satisfy the requirements of Article 253 (ex 190) (which requires that Regulations, Directives and Decisions shall state the reasons on which they are based), Community measures must set out clearly and concisely the facts and law which led the institution in question to adopt them. On the facts, the Court annulled parts of the Decision because of the inadequacy, vagueness and the inconsistency of the statement of reasons for the Decision.

Commission v Council Case 45/86

The Commission sought annulment of two Council Regulations on the grounds that the Regulations failed to specify a precise legal base.

Held The ECJ held that:

Community measures must include a statement of the facts and law which led the institution in question to adopt them, so as to make possible review by the Court and so that the Member States and the nationals concerned may have knowledge of the conditions under which the Community institutions have applied the Treaty.

3 Enforcement of Community Law – Article 226 EC (ex 169)

3.1 Commission discretion

Star Fruit Company v Commission Case 247/87

Star Fruit, a Belgian trader dealing in bananas, believed that a French regulation was contrary to Community law and asked the Commission to take action against France. When the Commission declined to deal with the issue, Star Fruit sought judicial review under Article 232 EC (ex 175), arguing that the Commission's failure to commence action under Article 226 EC (ex 169) was a failure to act.

Held The ECJ held that it is clear from Article 226 EC (ex 169) that the Commission has no obligation to act, but has complete discretion in deciding whether or not to exercise its powers under Article 226 EC (ex 169). Accordingly, the Commission's decision not to take action under Article 226 EC (ex 169) cannot be subject to challenge under Article 232 EC (ex 175).

Note ————————————————————————————————

It is worth noting that this means that individuals aggrieved by a breach of Community law cannot force the Commission to take any action.

———————————————————————————————————————

Lütticke (Alfons) GmbH v Commission Case 48/65

In similar facts to Case 247/87, above, Alfons Lütticke asked the Commission to proceed against Germany in respect of a levy imposed on imported milk powder, which he argued was contrary to Community law. The German authorities had since removed the levy and the Commission decided that it would not bring an action against Germany. The reason that Alfons Lütticke wanted the Commission to bring an Article 226 EC (ex 169) action was that he wanted to establish the infringement in order to claim damages in the German courts, because he had been adversely affected by the levy.

Held The ECJ held the Commission has complete discretion in relation to Article 226 EC (ex 169) proceedings.

3.1.1 The Commission can still institute proceedings where a Member State has rectified the breach

Commission v Italy (Re Ban on Pork Imports) Case 7/61

Italy prohibited the import of pork and the Commission commenced proceedings against the Italian State for infringement of Article 28 EC (ex 30). The Italian Government did not respond to the Commission's letter within the required time and so the Commission issued a reasoned opinion, giving Italy one month to put an end to the infringement.

Held If the Member State does not comply with the reasoned opinion within the time specified, the Commission has the right to bring the matter before the ECJ, even where the Member State has subsequently complied with the Commission's terms.

Commission v Greece Case 240/86

Held The ECJ confirmed its Decision in *Commission v Italy*, above. Even where a Member State has complied with a reasoned opinion after the period laid down by the Commission, the Commission still has an interest in pursuing the action. In particular, it may be important for those seeking redress in the national courts to establish that a Member State has failed to fulfil its obligations.

3.2 The reasoned opinion

Commission v Italy (Re Ban on Pork Imports) Case 7/61

The Commission wrote to the Italian State concerning an Italian decree which the Commission submitted was contrary to Community law. After giving Italy the opportunity to submit its observations as required by Article 226 (ex 169), the Commission sent a letter to Italy which requested that the infringement was brought to an end within one month. Italy did not comply with the request and the Commission brought the case before the ECJ. Italy challenged the proceedings on the basis that the letter did not constitute a reasoned opinion because it lacked adequate legal reasoning.

Held The ECJ held that the letter was a reasoned opinion; an opinion is a reasoned opinion when it contains a coherent statement of the reasons which convinced the Commission that the State in question had failed to fulfil one of its obligations under the Treaty.

Lütticke (Alfons) GmbH v Commission Case 48/65

For facts, see above, 3.1.

Held The ECJ held that the reasoned opinion issued by the Commission under Article 226 EC (ex 169) does not have binding effect and therefore cannot be subject to judicial review procedures under Article 230 (ex 173).

3.3 A Member State must be given adequate time to make its observations or to comply with the reasoned opinion

Commission v Ireland (Re Protection of Animal Health) Case 74/82

The Commission issued a reasoned opinion and gave Ireland five days to amend legislation which had stood on the Irish statute book for 40 years and which the Commission had not challenged since Ireland's accession to the Community.

Held The ECJ held in favour of the Commission. However, despite accepting such a short period of time, the Court criticised the Commission's action as unreasonable. The Court, in reaching its decision, took into account the fact that the Commission had waited for Ireland's observations before commencing legal proceedings before the Court.

Commission v Belgium Case 293/85

The ECJ held that the purpose of the pre-litigation procedure is to give the Member State concerned an opportunity to comply with its Community law obligations or the chance to defend itself against the complaints made by the Commission. Consequently, the Commission must allow Member States a reasonable period either to reply to the letter of formal notice, to comply with a reasoned opinion, or to prepare their defence. However, whether a period is reasonable depends upon the circumstances of the case and a very short period may sometimes be justified.

3.4 Time periods

Commission v France Case 7/71

This case involved the Commission bringing an action under Article 141 of the Euratom Treaty, but applies equally to the EC Treaty. The action was brought by the Commission against France in respect of an infringement that had been ongoing for six years. The French Government argued that the case should be dropped because of the long delay in bringing the action.

Held The ECJ held that an infringement action under Article 226 EC (ex 169) does not have to be brought within a predetermined period.

Commission v Netherlands Case C-96/89

In February 1984, the Commission sent a letter to the Dutch Government alleging an infringement of Community law. However, the Commission did not commence legal proceedings until March 1989, some five years later. The Commission stated that it had decided to delay proceedings until the outcome of another case before the ECJ.

Held The ECJ confirmed that there is no predetermined period within which the Commission must bring an action. On the facts before it, the ECJ held the delay had not prejudicially affected the Dutch Government's defence, therefore, the delay was not contrary to Article 226 EC (ex 169).

3.5   Defences

Commission v Italy Case 52/75
Not accepted In an action by the Commission against the Italian State, the Court refused to accept the argument put forward by Italy that other Member States had also failed to carry out their obligations by the required date.

Commission v Italy Case 30/72
Not accepted Italy sought to use the defence that a political crisis in Italy had effectively paralysed the Italian legislative procedure. This was not accepted by the ECJ as a valid defence.

Commission v UK Case 128/78
Not accepted The UK argued that its failure to comply with Community law obligations (it had failed to introduce legislation requiring the use of tachographs on certain vehicles) was justified for economic and practical reasons and, in particular, the opposition faced by the trade unions. As in the above two cases, the ECJ refused to accept this as a defence.

Commission v Germany (Re Nursing Directives) Case 29/84
The Commission brought an action against Germany for failure to implement two Directives concerning the qualification and training of nurses. The German Government argued that the action should be struck out on the grounds that the administrative practices and constitutional principles of German law were adequate implementation of the Directive.

Held The ECJ held that this was not sufficient. Implementation needs to be legally certain and clear.

Commission v Belgium Case 77/69
The Commission brought an action against Belgium in respect of a discriminatory tax on wood. The Belgian Government had shown itself willing to take steps to change the law but, due to the dissolution of the Belgian Parliament, the Government was unable to pass the law. The Belgian Government argued that it did not have the powers to pass the required legislation because of the separation of powers enshrined in the Belgian Constitution (the *force majeure* argument).

Held The ECJ held that this was not an acceptable defence.

Commission v Belgium Case 1/86

The Belgian Government failed to implement Directive 80/68 EEC on the protection of ground water against pollution. In its defence, the Belgian Government argued that the delay was caused as a result of institutional reforms which had resulted in a transfer of powers in respect of environmental matters to new regional authorities.

Held The ECJ held that a Member State cannot plead 'provisions, practices or circumstances existing in its internal legal system in order to justify a failure to comply' with Community law obligations.

Commission v Italy (Re Transport Statistics) Case 101/84

The Italian Government had not implemented a Directive and argued that the reason for its failure was that the data processing centre handling the implementation had been bombed. However, the delay in implementation was in fact a period of four and half years.

Held Although this might be regarded as a *force majeure* which could excuse non-implementation, on the facts, the delay of four and a half years was not excusable. Time had eroded the validity of the excuse.

Commission v France Case C-265/95

In this case, the Commission brought an action against France in respect of the French authorities' failure to take action against the French farmers' blockade of imported food, contrary to Article 28 EC (ex 30) of the Treaty. The French authorities argued that to take action against the demonstrators might have resulted in serious public order problems and even to social conflict.

Held This was no defence. Member States are under an obligation to observe Community law even where the State anticipates internal difficulties.

3.6   Article 243 EC (ex 186) – interim measures

Commission v UK Case C-246/89

This was the infringement action brought by the Commission in respect of the Merchant Shipping Act 1988, which was held to be in breach of Article 43 EC (ex 52) and which also resulted in the *Factortame* litigation. In this case before the ECJ, the Commission also asked the Court to make an interim order against the UK under Article 243 EC (ex 186). Under Article 243 EC (ex 186), the ECJ may, in any cases before it, prescribe any necessary interim measures, but these must not be ordered unless there are circumstances giving rise to urgency and the factual and legal grounds establish a *prima facie* case for the measures applied for.

Held There was a *prima facie* case against the UK. As regards the question of urgency, the test is whether it is necessary to grant interim relief in order to prevent serious and irreparable damage. The ECJ took the decision that this test was satisfied. Accordingly, the ECJ ordered that, pending the delivery of judgment in the case, the UK was required to suspend the application of the nationality requirements laid down in the Merchant Shipping Act 1988.

3.7 Article 227 EC (ex 170) – action by one Member State against another Member State

France v UK Case 141/78

This case concerned an Order in Council regulating the size of the mesh of fishing nets, as part of a fishery conservation policy. The French Government alleged that the UK measures were contrary to Community law.

Held The ECJ held in favour of France. The UK law was in breach of Community law.

4 Enforcement of Community Law – Articles 230 and 232 EC (ex 173 and 175)

4.1 Article 230 EC (ex 173) – which acts are reviewable?

Société Anonyme Cimeneries and Others v Commission (Re Noordwijks Cement Accord) Cases 8–11/66

Held A registered letter sent by a Commission official to an applicant was not an opinion, as argued by the Commission, but had the effect of a Decision and was, therefore, amenable to judicial review proceedings under Article 230 EC (ex 173). The letter stated that the company's immunity from fines was at an end and, accordingly, the Court stated that it had legal effect because it changed the legal position of the company.

Commission v Council (ERTA) Case 22/70

Discussions of the Council of Ministers concerning the attitude to be adopted by the (six) Member States at the negotiations of the European Road Transport Agreement (ERTA) were challenged by the Commission. The Commission alleged that the Council proceedings amounted to an encroachment by the Council on the Commission's area of responsibility. The Commission brought an action to annul the proceedings. The Council argued that the proceedings in question did not constitute an 'act' within the meaning of Article 230 EC (ex 173).

Held The proceedings in question were designed to lay down a course of action binding on both the institutions and the Member States: accordingly, they had legal effect and as such were amenable to judicial review. It would be wrong to restrict reviewable acts to those mentioned in Article 249 EC (ex 189).

International Business Machines v Commission Case 60/81

The Commission notified IBM, by means of a letter, that it had started investigative proceedings against IBM in order to discover whether the company was in breach of competition rules (Article 82 EC (ex 86)). Enclosed with the letter was a Statement of Objections and a request for the company's comments within a specified period.

Held The letter was not a reviewable act since it was merely a preparatory letter in the competition proceedings. However, the Court reiterated its case law on which acts are open to review:

> ... any measure the legal effects of which are binding on, and capable of affecting the interests of, the applicant by bringing about a distinct change in his legal position is an act or Decision which may be the subject of an action under Article 173 [now 230 EC] ... the form in which such acts or Decisions are cast is, in principle, immaterial as regards the question whether they are open to challenge ...

France v Commission (Re Pension Funds Communication) Case C-57/95

France challenged a Communication which had been issued by the Commission concerning pension funds. The Communication was drafted using imperative terms.

Held The ECJ held that the Commission Communication was intended to have legal effects and could, therefore, be challenged under Article 230 EC (ex 173).

4.1.1 Parliamentary acts are also subject to review

Parti Ecologiste Les Verts v European Parliament Case 294/83

The French Ecology Party sought the annulment of a Decision taken by the Parliamentary Bureau to award funding to a number of groups ostensibly to fund an information campaign prior to the parliamentary elections. The provisions of Article 230 EC (ex 173) under the Treaty of Rome (prior to amendment by the Single European Act 1986) did not refer to acts of the Parliament.

Held The ECJ held that Article 230 EC (ex 173) permitted the review of any measure of a Community instrument that could have binding effect. An interpretation of Article 230 EC (ex 173) which excluded measures adopted by the European Parliament from challenge would lead to a result contrary to the spirit of the Treaty. Consequently, measures adopted by the Parliament intended to have legal effect vis à vis third parties can be subject to an action for annulment.

Luxembourg v European Parliament Case 230/81

A Resolution of the Parliament to hold plenary sessions and committee meetings outside Luxembourg was challenged by Luxembourg.

Held The ECJ held that the resolution was a reviewable act. The justification was that the European Parliament is common to the three European Communities (EEC, ECSC and Euratom) and acts of the European Parliament are reviewable under the ECSC Treaty.

Note ————————————————————————————

The EC Treaty now clearly states, in Article 230 EC (ex 173), para 1, that the ECJ can review the legality of 'acts adopted jointly by the European

Parliament and the Council ... and acts of the European Parliament intended to produce legal effects vis à vis third parties'.

4.2 Who can bring judicial review proceedings – privileged applicants

4.2.1 The Member States

Italy v Commission Case 41/83

Italy challenged a Commission Decision addressed to British Telecom. The Decision stated that British Telecom was in breach of Article 82 EC (ex 86).

Held On the facts, the Court found in favour of the Commission, but there was no question about Italy's right to challenge the Decision: Member States are privileged applicants.

Italy v Council Case 166/78

Italy brought judicial review proceedings against a Council Decision concerning the premium payable to potato starch manufacturers, even though the Italian Minister had voted in favour of the Decision at the Council meeting that had adopted the Decision.

Held The ECJ held that Member States' use of Article 230 EC (ex 173) is not conditional upon them voting against the measure in question.

4.2.2 Position of the European Parliament

Parliament v Council (Re Comitology) Case 302/87

This case concerned the position of the European Parliament in judicial review proceedings. Article 230 EC (ex 173) of the Treaty does not give the Parliament the privileged status granted to the Council and the Commission. Here, the Parliament sought to establish that it had privileged status, particularly since parliamentary acts were amenable to review. (See *Parti Ecologiste*, above 4.1.1.) The ECJ held that the Parliament was neither a natural nor a legal person nor did it have privileged applicant status. The Parliament had no right to bring an action for annulment. (Although, see Advocate General Darmon's opinion that the Parliament should be given limited *locus standi* to defend its own prerogatives.)

Note ————————————————————————————
The ECJ modified its position in the following case.

Parliament v Council (Re Chernobyl) Case C-70/88

This case followed the *European Parliament v Council (Re Comitology)* case above. The Parliament once again sought to establish its right to bring judicial review proceedings and sought annulment of Council Regulation (Euratom) 3954/87. The Council had adopted this Regulation (following the disaster at the Chernobyl nuclear plant) under Article 31 of the Euratom Treaty, by virtue of which the Council only had to consult the Parliament. The Parliament argued that the Regulation should have been adopted under Article 100a (now 185 EC), which would have required adoption under the co-operation procedure (and hence a greater role for the Parliament).

Held In this case, the ECJ held that the Parliament has a right to bring an action for annulment providing that the action seeks only to safeguard the Parliament's prerogatives and providing the action is founded only on submission alleging their infringement.

Note ──────────────────────────────

This judicial Decision is now reflected in the Treaty as amended by the Treaty on European Union 1992. See Article 230 EC (ex 173), para 4.

European Parliament v Council (Re Aid to Bangladesh) Cases C-181 and 248/91

Here, the Parliament challenged a decision of the Member States meeting in Council (as opposed to a Council Decision) in respect of the aid programme to Bangladesh.

Held The Parliament had no *locus standi* since the decision had not infringed the prerogative power of the Parliament. Despite this, the ECJ went onto examine the claim and found the illegality proved.

4.3 Non-privileged applicants – natural and legal persons – reviewable acts

Gibraltar v Council Case C-298/89

Held A 'natural or legal person' includes a State which is not a Member State of the Community. Gibraltar fell into this category.

4.3.1 A Decision addressed to another person

Plaumann & Co v Commission Case 25/62

P imported clementines into Germany from outside the Community and was charged a customs duty of 13% in conformity with the Common Customs Tariff. The German Government sought authorisation from the Commission to reduce the duty to 10%, but the Commission refused permission. P sought annulment of the Commission's Decision, addressed to Germany. The question for the Court was whether a Decision addressed to a Member State could constitute a 'Decision addressed to another person'.

Held A Decision addressed to a Member State can be regarded as a Decision addressed to another person.

4.3.2 A Decision that takes the form of a Regulation – a Regulation will not be a Decision when it applies to persons generally

Zuckerfabrik Watenstedt GmbH v Council Case 6/68
This case involved a challenge by Z to a Council Regulation. The Regulation terminated price maintenance for producers of raw sugar beet with effect from a prescribed date. It affected fewer than 30 producers.

Held The ECJ held that a measure does not lose its character as a Regulation simply because it may be possible to ascertain the number, or even identity, of the persons to which it applies at a given time, as long as there is no doubt that the measure is applicable as the result of an objective situation, that is, it affects all present and potential sugar beet producers.

Calpak SpA v Commission Cases 789 and 790/90
C, an Italian company, sought annulment of Regulations providing aid for the production of Williams' pears preserved in syrup. The level of aid was established according to production in a year when Italian production had been low. Calpak argued that the Regulation affected an identifiable category of which he was one.

Held The ECJ held that the measure applied to an objectively determined situation and produced legal effects for 'categories of persons described in a generalised and abstract manner'. A Regulation cannot be called into question by the mere fact that it is possible to determine the number or even the identity of the producers affected by it.

4.3.3 A Regulation will be a Decision when it applies to fixed and ascertainable persons

International Fruit Company v Commission Cases 41–44/70
The IFC was a company involved in importing apples and had applied for an import licence. The number of licences available in a given period was stipulated in a Commission Regulation. The Commission was responsible for deciding how many licences were to be issued on the basis of information received from the Member States about the applications received in the previous week. IFC were not granted a licence.

Held The ECJ held that the contested Regulation was not a provision of general application within the meaning of Article 249 EC (ex 189). The Court decided that the Regulation was in fact a 'conglomeration of individual Decisions' taken by the Commission under the guise of a Regulation. Each Decision affected a fixed and closed class of persons (being those that had made the applications in the previous week). The class was fixed and closed because no new licence application could be added. Consequently, each Decision affected the legal position of each licence applicant.

Note ──
The question of whether a Regulation is really a Decision and whether applicants are able to satisfy the test of individual concern are very similar – see *Plaumann & Co v Commission*, below, 4.4.
──

Confédération Nationale des Producteurs et Légumes v Council Cases 16 and 17/62

The Confederation (a French association of fruit and vegetable producers) sought annulment of a Council Regulation. A natural or legal person can only contest a Regulation if it is, in essence, a Decision.

Held The ECJ held that the Court can not be restricted to considering the official title of the measure. 'The essential characteristics of a Decision arise from the limitation of the persons to whom it is addressed.' In cases where there is doubt as to whether a measure is a Regulation or a Decision, it is necessary to ascertain whether the measure in question is of direct and individual concern to specific individuals.

Extramet Industrie SA v Council Case C-358/899

Held The fundamental characteristic of a Regulation is that it is applicable to objectively determined situations and that it involves legal consequences for categories of persons viewed in a general and abstract manner.

4.4   Individual concern

Plaumann & Co v Commission Case 25/62

P imported clementines into Germany from outside the Community and was charged a customs duty of 13% in conformity with the Common Customs Tariff. The German Government sought authorisation from the Commission to reduce the duty to 10% but the Commission refused permission. P sought annulment of the Commission's Decision, addressed to Germany.

The ECJ, in determining whether P was individually concerned by the Decision, laid down the following test:

Persons other than those to whom a Decision is addressed may only claim to be individually concerned if that Decision affects them by reason of certain attributes which are peculiar to them or by reason of circumstances in which they are differentiated from all other persons and by virtue of these factors distinguishes them individually just as in the case of the person addressed.

P was not individually concerned. On the facts, P was affected by the disputed decision as an importer of clementines, 'that is to say, by reason of a commercial activity which may at any time be practised by any person'. P was not distinguished in any way.

Töpfer (Alfred) KG v Commission Cases 106–07/63

The Commission took a Decision fixing the levy on maize imported into Germany, with effect from 2 October. Töpfer had applied for a licence to import maize into Germany on 1 October. The German Government rejected Töpfer's application and then the German authorities sought retrospective approval from the Commission. The Commission issued a Decision retrospectively authorising Germany to refuse applications for import licences made between 1 and 4 October. Töpfer challenged this Commission Decision.

Held The only persons who were affected by the Commission Decision were importers who had applied for an import licence on 1 October . The number and identity of these importers had already become fixed and it was possible to identify them before the 4 October when the contested Decision was taken. The Commission was in a position to know that its Decision affected the interests and the position of these identifiable importers. Thus, these importers, including Töpfer, were differentiated from all other importers. They were, therefore, individually concerned.

Note
This was one of the very rare occasions when a non-privileged applicant has managed to demonstrate direct and individual concern.

Spijker (Kwasten) BV v Commission (Re Chinese Brushes) Case 231/82

This case involved a Commission Decision which authorised three Member States to suspend application of the common commercial tariff to the import of brushes from China from a prescribed date. This Decision was challenged by S, the sole importer into the three States and whose application had in fact prompted the authorisation:

The contested Decision concerns the applicant merely by virtue of its objective capacity as an importer of the goods in question in the same manner as any other trader, who is or might be in the future, in the same situation.

Held The Decision was of general application covering situations which are determined objectively and therefore not of individual concern to S.

Werner A Bock KG v Commission (Re Chinese Mushrooms) Case 62/70

The German Government applied to the Commission for authorisation to block imports of Chinese mushrooms into Germany. Authorisation was granted by the Commission. Bock, who had applied for a permit to import Chinese mushrooms, had been told by the German authorities that they would refuse his application as soon as they were authorised by the Commission. Bock challenged the Commission Decision.

Held The ECJ held that Bock was individually concerned. When the Commission took the Decision, it was aware of Bock's application and aware that the Decision would result in Bock's application being refused.

4.5 Direct concern

A measure will be of direct concern to the applicant if it leaves the State no real discretion in implementation.

Società Éridania Zuccherifici Nazionali v Commission Cases 10 and 18/68

A sugar refining company challenged three Commission Decisions which granted aid to one of it's competitors. The Decision had named the companies concerned.

Held The applicants were not directly concerned. Although the Decision had named the companies concerned and authorised the granting of aid, the actual allocation of the grant aid was made by the Italian Government. The matter was within the Member State's discretion and, therefore, the applicants were not directly concerned.

Note ————

In these circumstances, the company should have brought an action against the Italian State in respect of the way it had exercised its discretion concerning the grant allocation.

ARPOSOL v Council Case 55/86

ARPOSOL, a Spanish fishing association, sought the annulment of Council Regulation (EEC) 3781/85. Under the Council Regulation, Spanish fishing vessels which had infringed Community fishing rules could be removed from the list of vessels authorised to fish in Community waters.

Held The ECJ held that the association was not directly concerned, its members were affected only by the national decision to remove the names from the list and that decision was later confirmed by the Commission.

Alcan Aluminium Raeren SA v Commission Case 69/69

The Commission issued a Decision to Belgium and Luxembourg refusing to allow imports of unwrought aluminum at a reduced levy. The Decision was challenged by Alcan, an aluminum company and importer.

Held The ECJ held that Alcan was not directly concerned because the two Member States were free to choose how they implemented the distribution of the quota.

Piraiki-Patraiki v Commission Case 11/82

At the request of the French Government, the Commission authorised France to apply quotas on certain imports of yarn from Greece. This was challenged by Greek manufacturers and exporters who had entered in contracts to export yarn to France in amounts in excess of the quota. The exporters could not fulfil their contractual obligations because of the quota.

Held The ECJ held that those Greek traders with prior contractual obligations were directly concerned. The Decision was annulled insofar as it applied to contracts entered into before the date of the notification of the Decision. The Court held that the plaintiffs were directly concerned by the Commission Decision (as opposed to any national implementing measures) because the possibility that the French authorities might not take advantage of the Commission authorisation was entirely theoretical, since there could be no doubt as to the intention of the French authorities to apply the Decision.

Werner A Bock AG v Commission (Re Chinese Mushrooms) Case 62/70
For facts, see 4.4, above.

Held The ECJ held that the matter was of direct concern to the applicant. In theory, the German Government had discretion whether or not to use the authorisation. However, the German Government had told B that it would reject his application as soon as the Commission had granted it the requisite permission, and it had requested authorisation from the Commission with Bock's application in mind. The ECJ therefore considered that he was directly concerned.

Metro-SB-Grossmärkte GmbH and Co KG v Commission (No 1) Case 26/76
As a result of being excluded from a distribution network for a company called SABA, Metro complained to the Commission (under Article 3 of Regulation (EEC) 17/62) that SABA was acting contrary to Article 81 EC (ex 85). However, the Commission took a Decision that SABA had not breached Article 81 EC (ex 85). Metro challenged the Commission's Decision, which was addressed to SABA.

Held The ECJ held that a company which has a right to ask the Commission, under Regulation (EEC) 17/62, to investigate violations of the competition rules, should be able, if their request is not complied with, to institute proceedings under Article 230 EC (ex 173). Metro was held to be directly and individually concerned.

4.6   Anti-dumping cases

NTN Toyo Bearing Co Ltd and Others v Council (Re Japanese Ball-bearings) Cases 113/77 and 118–21/77
A Council Regulation imposed an anti-dumping duty on ball-bearings originating in Japan. This was challenged by NTN, a Japanese ball-bearing manufacturer, and a number of other major ball-bearing manufacturers.

Held The ECJ held that four of the manufacturers were directly and individually concerned because the Regulation had expressly referred to them.

Extramet Industrie SA v Council Case C-358/89

Extramet was a French company that sought annulment of a Regulation which imposed an anti-dumping duty on the imports of calcium metal from China and the Soviet Union. The company was not involved in the proceedings leading up to the anti-dumping Regulation.

Held Measures imposing anti-dumping duties may, without losing their character as Regulations, be of individual concern to certain traders. This would be the case where the traders were identified in the measure. But it could also include other traders by reason of certain attributes which are peculiar to them and which differentiate them from all other persons. On the facts, Extramet was held to be individually concerned because it was the largest importer of the product and also the end-user of the product: its business activities depended to a very large extent on these imports. They were 'seriously affected' by the Regulation in view of the limited number of manufacturers of the product and the difficulties the company would encounter in obtaining supplies from the main producer, who was also the company's main competitor.

Note

This represents a departure from the Court's previous case law and something of a more liberal approach to standing.

4.6.1   A new more liberal approach to standing?

Codorniu SA v Council Case C-309/89

Codorniu was a Spanish producer of quality sparkling wine. The Council enacted Regulation (EEC) 2045/89 which restricted the use of the term 'crémant' to certain quality wines originating in France and Luxembourg. Codorniu had registered a trade mark for the term 'Gran Crémant de Codorniu' in Spain in 1942. The company alleged that the Regulation was really a Decision, in that it affected a well determined class of producers who, on 1 September 1989, traditionally designated their sparkling wine as crémant. The company alleged that the direct result of the Regulation would be to prevent it from using the term crémant and this would result in a loss of 38% of its turnover.

Held The Court reaffirmed its position that the general application of a Regulation is not called into question by the fact that it is possible to determine more or less exactly the number or even identity of the persons affected, so long as it applies to them by virtue of an objective legal or factual situation. However, by reserving the right to use the term for French and Luxembourg producers, the Regulation prevented Codurniu from using its graphic trade mark. Codurniu were held to be individually concerned. The Regulation was subsequently held to be void.

Note ──

The Court appears to be adopting a more liberal stance in this case, indicating that a Regulation will be of individual concern to an applicant if it has serious economic consequences for him.

──

4.6.2   The position of interest groups

Associazone Italiana Tenico Economica del Cemento (AITEC) v Commission Cases T-447–49/93

In this case, the Italian and British Trade Associations of cement producers challenged a Commission Decision which was addressed to the Greek Government. The Decision approved the award of State aid to a Greek cement manufacturer. The question was whether the associations were directly and individually concerned.

Held The Court of First Instance held that the Associations had *locus standi*. The Court stated that a trade association would be allowed to bring an action against a Decision where the association represented the individual interests of some of its members whilst, at the same time, protecting the interests of all of its members. The Court held that, on the facts of the case, 'collective action brings procedural advantages'. The Commission Decision was annulled.

Federolio v Commission Case T-122/96

Held The Court of First Instance held that an association would be granted *locus standi* in the following circumstances:

- the trade association has been expressly granted procedural rights;
- the trade association represents the individuals or undertakings which themselves have *locus standi*; or
- the trade association itself is affected.

Stichting Greenpeace Council v Commission Case C-321/95P

This case involved an appeal from the Court of First Instance to the ECJ. The applicants were seeking annulment of a Commission Decision to allocate regional structural funds to Spain in respect of the construction of two power stations in the Canary Islands. The applicants, an environmental pressure group, argued that in reaching this Decision the Commission had breached Community environmental laws (namely, the Environmental Assessment Directive 85/337/EEC). The Court of First Instance ruled that Greenpeace were not individually concerned. Greenpeace argued before the ECJ that this left a 'legal vacuum in ensuring compliance with Community environmental legislation', since environmental interests are shared in common by very large numbers of people so that there can never be a closed class of people.

Held The Court dismissed the appeal. The specific situation of the applicant (the pressure group) was not taken into account when the Commission made its Decision. Similarly, the Decision affected the applicant in a general and abstract fashion, like any other person in the same situation. Therefore, Greenpeace were not individually concerned.

4.7 Grounds for review

4.7.1 Lack of competence

Germany, France, Netherlands, Denmark and UK v Commission Joined Cases 281, 283–85 and 287/85
This was an action brought by Germany and a number of other Member States against the Commission. The Member States, concerned about the Commission's migration policy towards non-Member States, issued a Decision which set up a consultation procedure on these policies. The Commission based its Decision on Article 118 (now 137 EC) of the Treaty and the Member States challenged the Commission's competence to take such action.
Held The ECJ held that Article 118 (now 137 EC) allowed such action to be taken and stated that the Commission had the power to take a legally binding Decision in this area. (See above, 1.2.2.)

Meroni & Co, Industrie Metallurgische SpA v ECSC High Authority Case 9/56
M challenged a Decision taken by the High Authority to delegate certain powers to agencies, contending the High Authority did not have the power to do this.
Held The ECJ held that the High Authority had such powers, providing it recognised that the delegation was necessary to achieve the aims laid down in the Treaty. A delegation of power also had to be subject to clearly defined objective criteria.

Note ─────────────────────────────────
This case was heard in 1956. The High Authority no longer exists: its functions have been transferred to the European Commission.

4.7.2 Infringement of an essential procedural requirement

Commission v Council Case 45/86
The Commission challenged two Regulations adopted by the Council on the basis that they failed to identify their legislative bases. Article 253 EC (ex 190) of the Treaty provides that Regulations, Directives and Decisions shall state the reasons on which they are based.

Held Failure to give reasons for Community acts, as required by Article 253 EC (ex 190) of the Treaty, is a breach of an essential procedural requirement. On the facts, it was held that the Council had not satisfied this requirement and the Regulations were annulled.

Roquette Frères SA v Council Case 138/79

RF challenged a Council Regulation on the grounds that the Regulation had been adopted by the Council without the consultation of the Parliament, as required under Article 37 EC (ex 43) of the Treaty.

Held The ECJ held that the consultation procedure is an essential procedural requirement, being the means by which the Parliament plays a part in the legislative process. Breach of such an essential procedure rendered the Regulation void.

4.7.3 Infringement of the Treaty, or of any rule of law relating to its application

Nold KG v Commission Case 4/73

N, a German coal wholesale company, challenged a Commission Decision under the ECSC Treaty. The Decision made it impossible for N to purchase from his supplier because he could not fulfil the prescribed minimum purchase requirements. N claimed that the Decision, by depriving it of direct supplies, violated the company's fundamental rights. (For further discussion, see Chapter 9.)

Held Fundamental rights form an integral part of the general principles of Community law. However, on the facts of the case, the Decision did not breach such rights.

4.7.4 Misuse of power

Fabrique de Fer de Charleroi v Commission Cases 351 and 360/85

F claimed that the Commission had misused its powers under Article 58 ECSC Treaty in that it had given special treatment to the only Danish steel-maker under the steel quota system. F contended that the powers had been exercised, not for their proper purpose, but in order to ensure the survival of the only steel producer in Denmark

Held The Commission had misused its powers. It had taken into account considerations which were not laid down in the relevant provisions of the Treaty.

Franco Giuffrida v Council Case 105/75

This was a staff dispute. Two officials, Franco Giuffrida and Martino, were competing for a promotion in Community services. FG argued that the competition was in reality a sham in order to enable M to get the job.

Found The ECJ found in FG's favour. They stated that this was a misuse of power because the recruitment procedures had been used for the wrong purposes.

4.8   Article 232 EC (ex 175) – action for failure to act

Società 'Eridania' Zuccherifici Nazionali v Commission Cases 10 and 18/68
The Society had previously sought to challenge three Commission Decisions under Article 230 EC (ex 173), but had failed to prove direct and individual concern. The Society then brought an action under Article 232 EC (ex 175), arguing that the Commission's failure to revoke the Decisions amounted to a failure to act.

Held The ECJ held that Article 232 EC (ex 175) is intended to establish an illegal omission. Article 232 EC (ex 175) proceedings can not be used when there are other methods of recourse, such as Article 230 EC (ex 173). To use Article 232 EC (ex 175) in such circumstances, would allow a method of recourse parallel to that of Article 230 EC (ex 173), but which would not be subject to the same conditions, such as the strict time limits laid down in the Treaty.

4.9   Relationship between Articles 230 and 234 EC (ex 173 and 177)

Alusuisse v Council and Commission Case 307/81
A group of importers sought to challenge an anti-dumping Regulations.

Held The ECJ held that the importers could not use the review procedures under Article 230 EC (ex 173) (they were not directly and individually concerned). The ECJ stated that 'importers may contest before the national courts individual measures taken by national authorities in application of Community Regulations'.

TWD Textilwerke Deggendorf GmbH v Bundesrepublik Deutschland Case C-188/92
The Commission issued a Decision to Germany stating that the aid that the German authorities had granted to TWD, a textile company, was contrary to the Treaty and had to be repaid. The company was advised, by the German authorities, that it had the right to challenge the Commission Decision under Article 230 EC (ex 173). Since the company was expressly named in the Commission Decision, it would have been able to prove direct and individual concern. However, TWD failed to bring an action within the prescribed time limits. The company then, at a later date, sought to challenge the validity of the Commission Decision in the course of proceedings before the national courts.

Held The Commission refused to give a preliminary ruling on the validity of the Decision (under Article 234 EC (ex 177)) on the grounds that the company clearly knew about its rights under Article 230 EC (ex 173) and had failed to take them up.

R v Intervention Board for Agricultural Produce ex p Accrington Beef Co Ltd Case C-241/95

In this case, the applicants challenged the validity of a Regulation during judicial review proceedings before the English courts. A preliminary ruling was sought on the validity of the Regulation.

Held The ECJ held that the challenge was admissible even though the applicant had failed to bring a direct action under Article 230 EC (ex 173) within the time limit. The Court recognised that it was not clear that the applicants would have been directly or individually concerned.

5 Indirect Enforcement of Community Law through the National Courts

5.1 The preliminary rulings procedure – purpose

Costa v ENEL Case 6/64

C sought a declaration from the Italian court that he was not obliged to pay his electricity bill (less than £2!) on the grounds that the Italian law which had nationalised the electricity industry in 1962 and created the new company, ENEL, was contrary to certain provisions of the EEC Treaty, including Article 37 (now 31 EC). The Italian court sought a preliminary ruling on the relevant Community law provisions. However, the Italian Government intervened once the matter was referred to the ECJ and argued that the application for a preliminary ruling was wholly inadmissible because the dispute involved matters of national law unconnected with the Treaty.

Held The ECJ held that the EEC Treaty has created its own legal system which has become an integral part of the legal systems in all the Member States and which the national courts are bound to apply. As such, Article 234 EC (ex 177) is to be applied, regardless of any domestic law, whenever questions relating to the interpretation of the Treaty arise.

Kledingverkoopbedrijf De Geus en Uitdenbogerd v Robert Bosch GmbH Case 13/61

This was the first case submitted to the ECJ under the Article 234 EC (ex 177) procedure. Advocate General Lagrange, in his opinion to the Court, stated:

> The progressive integration of the Treaty into the legal, social and economic life of the Member States must involve more and more frequently the application and, when the occasion arises, the interpretation of the Treaty in municipal litigation … the provisions of Article 177 [now 234 EC] must lead to a real and fruitful co-operation between the municipal courts and the Court of Justice.

Rheinmühlen-Düsseldorf v Einführ und Vorratsstelle für Getreide und Futtermittel (No 1) Case 166/73

Held The ECJ held that:

> Article 177 [now 234 EC] is essential for the preservation of the Community character of the law established by the Treaty and has the object of ensuring that in all circumstances this law is the same in all States of the Community.

Stauder v Stadt Ulm Case 29/69

Different language translations of Council Decision (69/71/EEC) resulted in different meanings. A preliminary ruling was sought to find out the correct Community interpretation.

Held It is impossible to consider one version of a text in isolation but texts must be interpreted on the basis of the author's intention, and the purpose of the provision, in the light of the versions in all languages.

Marianne Worsdorfer v Raad van Arbeid Case 9/79

A Dutch court sought a preliminary ruling on the meaning of a particular word in a Regulation which appeared to apply only to a females.

Held The ECJ held that the interpretation of a provision of Community law must not be made in isolation, but must be interpreted and applied in the light of the versions existing in other official languages. Other versions of the same Regulation made it clear that the particular provision related to both men and women.

Note ————

The ECJ is well placed to give an interpretation of Community law. Look at Lord Bingham's remarks in *Commissioners of Customs and Excise v Samex* (1983), below, 5.6.

5.2   The scope of the preliminary rulings procedure

5.2.1   Interpretation

Article 234 EC (ex 177) extends to non-binding acts

Grimaldi v Fonds des Maladies Professionnelles Case C-322/88

A Belgian tribunal sought a preliminary ruling concerning an EC Recommendation.

Held The ECJ held that its jurisdiction under Article 234 EC (ex 177) enabled it to give preliminary rulings on the interpretation and validity of all acts adopted by the institutions, including Recommendations.

Article 234 EC (ex 177) also gives the ECJ jurisdiction to give rulings in respect of certain agreements with non-Member States

Amministrazione delle Finanze dello Stato v Società Petrolifera Italiana SpA Cases 267–69/81

The ECJ was asked to give a preliminary ruling on the effect within the Community of the General Agreement on Tariffs and Trade (GATT).

Held The provisions of the GATT should, like all other agreements binding the Community, receive uniform interpretation and are amenable to the preliminary rulings procedure.

5.2.2   Validity

International Chemical Corporation SpA v Amministrazione delle Finanze dello Stato Case 66/80

An Italian court sought a preliminary ruling on whether an earlier ECJ judgment, declaring a Council Regulation void, was effective in any later litigation.

Held Although a judgment of the ECJ under Article 234 EC (ex 177) declaring a Regulation void is only directly addressed to the national court which sought the ruling, it is 'sufficient reason' for any other national court to regard that Regulation as void. However, this does not deprive national courts of the right to raise the question again under the preliminary rulings procedure.

National courts must seek a reference when validity of Community measures is raised

Foto-Frost v Hauptzollamt Lübeck Ost Case 314/85

In proceedings before a German court, the applicant asked the national court to declare a Commission Decision invalid. The German court sought a preliminary ruling on whether a national court can declare a Community measure invalid on the grounds that it was in breach of a Community Regulation.

Held A national court can declare a Community measure valid but it does not have the power to declare acts of the Community institutions invalid. Where the issue of the invalidity of a provision of EC law is raised, the national court must seek a preliminary ruling.

The ECJ cannot rule on the compatibility of national law with Community law

NV Algemene Transport-en Expeditie Onderneming Van Gend en Loos v Nederlandse Administratie der Belastingen Case 26/62

For facts, see below, 6.1.1.

Held The ECJ held that it has no jurisdiction to rule on the comparability of domestic law with EC law.

5.3 Which courts or tribunals can seek a preliminary ruling?

5.3.1 Any court or tribunal may seek a ruling – courts with discretion

Pretore di Salo v Persons Unknown Case 14/86

Held The ECJ held that the Italian *pretore*, which combines the functions of a public prosecutor and an examining magistrate, could seek a preliminary ruling. The ECJ has jurisdiction to provide preliminary rulings if the request comes from a:

> ... court or tribunal which has acted in the general framework of its task of judging, independently and in accordance with law, cases coming within the jurisdiction conferred by law, even though certain functions of that court or tribunal ... are not, strictly speaking, of a judicial nature.

Broekmeulen v Huisarts Registratie Commissie Case 246/80

Held A Dutch medical appeal committee was held to be a court or tribunal for the purposes of Article 234 EC (ex 177). In the practical absence of an effective means of redress before the ordinary courts, in a matter concerning the application of Community law, the appeal committee was held to have jurisdiction to seek a ruling. The appeal committee operated with the consent and co-operation of the public authorities and, after an adversarial procedure, delivered decisions which were final.

Nordsee Deutsche Hochseefischerei GmbH v Reederei Mond Hochseefischerei Nordstern AG and Co Case 102/81

Held An arbitrator appointed under a private contract was not a court or tribunal within the meaning of Article 234 EC (ex 177), even where there was no recourse to the ordinary courts. This was because arbitration is not mandatory and also because the public authorities were not directly or indirectly involved or associated with the arbitration proceedings. There must be some link between the arbitration procedure and the ordinary court system.

5.3.2 Court's discretion to refer not fettered by national rules

Rheinmühlen Düsseldorf v Einführ und Vorratsstelle für Getreide und Futtermittel (No 1) Case 166/73

A preliminary ruling was sought specifically on the question of whether Article 234(2) EC (ex 177(2)) gives courts or tribunals a completely unfettered discretion as to whether to refer, or whether they are bound by precedent or rules of higher courts.

Held National courts have the widest discretion in referring matters to the ECJ if they consider that a case raises questions of interpretation or consideration of the validity of Community law. The purpose of Article 234 EC (ex 177) is to ensure that Community law, in all circumstances, is the same in all Member States and national rules cannot undermine this:

> It follows ... that a rule of national law whereby a court is bound on points of law by the rulings of a superior court cannot deprive the inferior courts of their power to refer.

5.4 The obligation to refer – what is meant by a 'court from which there is no judicial remedy'?

Costa v ENEL Case 6/64

For facts, see above, 5.1. The case was heard by the Italian magistrates because of the very small sum of money involved. There was no right of appeal against the magistrates' decision.

Held The ECJ held that even an inferior court, such as the magistrates' court, could be a court from which there is no judicial remedy under Article 234(3) EC (ex 177(3)) where, as in this case, there is no right of appeal.

Bulmer (HP) Ltd v J Bollinger SA (1974)

Bollinger, the champagne makers, asserted that the word 'champagne' could only be used in relation to champagne produced in the Champagne region of France. Bulmer, a cider manufacturer, marketed a cider called 'champagne cider'. Bollinger asked the Divisional Court to seek a preliminary ruling from the ECJ, but the court refused and Bollinger appealed to the Court of Appeal on a point of law. The Court of Appeal upheld the decision of the lower court. Lord Denning stated that, 'short of the House of Lords, no other English court is bound to refer a question to the European Court'.

(However, note Stephenson and Stamp LJJ left the matter open.)

Hagen v Moretti (1980)

In a case concerning patent law, Buckley LJ in the Court of Appeal held that, if leave to appeal to the House of Lords is refused, the Court of Appeal becomes a court from which there is no judicial remedy and falls under Article 234(3) EC (ex 177(3)).

Magnavision v General Optical Council (No 2) (1987)

Following conviction under the Opticians Act 1958, Magnavision appealed to the High Court on a point of law. The Queen's Bench Division rejected an argument that the provisions of the Act were in breach of Article 28 EC (ex 30) and refused leave to appeal to the House of Lords. There is no right of appeal against the Divisional Court's refusal to grant leave in criminal cases.

It was then argued on behalf of the plaintiff that, since the High Court had refused leave to appeal it had become the final court and was thus bound to seek a preliminary ruling. (The High Court had refused to seek a ruling during the proceedings on the basis that the relevant Community law was clear.) The High Court dismissed this argument and refused to seek a preliminary ruling on the particular question as to whether the Divisional Court became a court from which there is no judicial remedy if it refused leave to appeal to the House of Lords.

R v Pharmaceutical Society of Great Britain ex p the Association of Pharmaceutical Importers (1987)

In this case, the Association of Pharmaceutical Importers challenged a UK law relating to the dispensing of certain brands of medicine. The Association alleged the UK law breached Article 28 EC (ex 30). Although the Court of Appeal sought a preliminary ruling on the issue, in an *obiter* statement, Kerr LJ said:

> A court or tribunal below the House of Lords can only fall within the last paragraph [of Article 177 (now 234 EC)] where there is no possibility of any further appeal from it.

5.5 When will it be necessary to seek a reference?

CILFIT Srl v Italian Ministry of Health Case 283/81

C, an Italian company involved in the import of wool from other EC Member States, contested the legality of a health inspection levy imposed by the Ministry of Health on wool imports. The Italian court considered that Community law on the matter was clear. However, because it was a court of final instance, it was uncertain as to whether it was obliged to seek a preliminary ruling. The Italian court therefore sought a preliminary ruling on whether it was obliged to refer the matter to the ECJ in circumstances where the relevant Community law was clear and precise.

Held National courts from which there is no judicial remedy, that is, courts of final instance (such as the House of Lords) are not required to submit a matter to the ECJ if the Community law at issue is not necessary to enable them to give judgment. The ECJ held that a reference will not be necessary where:

(1) the question of EC law is irrelevant;

(2) the question has already been decided by the ECJ; or

(3) '... the correct application of Community law may be so obvious as to leave no scope for any reasonable doubt as to the manner in which the question is to be resolved.'

However, national courts must, before reaching this conclusion, be convinced that the matter is equally obvious to the courts of the other Member States and the ECJ and courts must also bear in mind the particular characteristics of Community law.

Da Costa en Schaake and Others v Nederlandse Belastingadministratie Cases 28–30/62

Held No national court can be deprived of the opportunity to seek a ruling on a provision of Community law that has already been interpreted by the ECJ. In this particular case, the ECJ said there was no ground for giving a new interpretation of Article 25 EC (ex 12) from that already given in *NV Algemene Transport-en Expeditie Onderneming Van Gend en Loos v Nederlandse Administratie der Belastingen* Case 26/62 (see Chapters 7 and 10).

5.6   Approach of the English courts

Bulmer (HP) Ltd v Bollinger SA (1974)

Lord Denning in the Court of Appeal gave the following guidelines on whether a decision on a question was 'necessary'. He stated that a reference would only be necessary if it were conclusive to the judgment. It would not be necessary if:

- there has been no previous ruling from the ECJ; or
- the provisions in question are *acte clair* (literally meaning 'act clear').

Lord Denning also suggested that a national court should consider the length of time that it takes to receive a preliminary ruling, the expense and the importance of the point, as well as the wishes of the parties to the proceedings.

Lord Denning's judgment also includes the following statement;

> Unless the point is really difficult and important, it would seem better for the English judge to decide it himself.

Note ———

Note the difference between this test and that laid down by the ECJ in the *CILFIT* case (see above, 5.5). The test laid down by Lord Denning is more restrictive than that prescribed by the ECJ.

Commissioners of Customs and Excise v Samex Aps (1983)

Samex Aps entered into a contract to buy goods from a non-Member State. Samex had obtained an import licence which stated that the imports had to be made before a certain deadline. The Customs and Excise authorities found that the goods had been imported after that date. Samex argued, by way of defence, that the customs authorities were in breach of a relevant

EC Regulation and asked the court to seek a preliminary ruling. The company's argument that a preliminary ruling should be sought was accepted by Bingham LJ.

Held Bingham LJ stated that the ECJ has a 'panoramic view of the Community and its institutions, a detailed knowledge of the Treaties and of much subordinate legislation made under them ... which no national judge denied the collective experience of the Court of Justice could hope to achieve'. Bingham LJ went on to say that the ECJ, in a variety of situations, is very much better placed to assess the meaning and interpretation of Community law than a national court. This is a much more flexible approach than that adopted by Denning LJ in *HP Bulmer Ltd v Bollinger SA* (1974).

Equal Opportunities Commission v Secretary of State for Employment (1994)

The EOC brought this case against the Secretary of State for Employment, arguing that legislation which required part time workers to work for five years before qualifying for redundancy pay or unfair dismissal compensation was in breach of Article 141 EC (ex 119) (because most part time workers are women). The House of Lords did not refer the matter to the ECJ because it said that the position in EC law was so clear and the Lords ruled that the provisions of the domestic legislation were unlawful.

R v International Stock Exchange ex p Else (1982) Ltd (1993)

In this case, Sir Bingham MR (as he was then) said in an *obiter* statement:

I understand the correct approach in principle of a national court (other than a final court of appeal) to be quite clear; if the facts have been found and the Community law issue is crucial to the court's final decision, the appropriate course is ordinarily to refer the issue to the Court of Justice unless the national court can with complete confidence resolve the issue.

Chiron Corporation v Murex Diagnostics Ltd (1995)

In the Court of Appeal, Balcombe LJ stated:

Where there is no right even to apply to the House of Lords for leave to appeal from a decision of the Court of Appeal – for example, on a refusal by the Court of Appeal for leave to appeal against the decision of the court below, or a refusal by the Court of Appeal, on a renewed application, to grant leave to apply for judicial review – then the Court of Appeal will be the court of last resort. So Lord Denning stated the matter too widely.

5.7   Procedural issues

Irish Creamery Milk Suppliers Association v Government of Ireland Cases 36 and 71/80

In this case, the plaintiffs argued that an Irish levy on certain agricultural products was contrary to the Treaty. The Irish Government sought to delay the timing of the reference until the facts of the case had been fully established. The Irish court, in addition to seeking an interpretation of the relevant Treaty provisions, also asked the ECJ at what stage in the proceedings a preliminary ruling should be sought.

Held On the question of when to seek a preliminary ruling, the ECJ held that, in certain circumstances, it might be convenient to establish the facts and questions of purely national law before seeking a ruling. However, the Court asserted that it is entirely for the national court to determine at which stage in the proceedings to seek a preliminary ruling, dictated by considerations of procedural organisation and efficiency.

Fratelli Pardini SpA v Ministero del Commercio con l'Estero Case 338/85

Held The ECJ held that the ECJ has no jurisdiction to give a ruling if the proceedings before the national court have finished.

The nature of the question

Pretore Di Salo v Persons Unknown Case 146/86

Held The question referred from the Italian magistrate (the *pretore*) was too general to answer. However, the court may extract from the wording of a question those elements which concern the interpretation of Community law.

5.8   Refusal to give a preliminary ruling

Foglia v Novello (No 1) Case 104/79

F and N were in a contractual dispute over a duty paid on the import of wine from Italy to France. On the facts, it appeared that the dispute was contrived by the parties in order to obtain a preliminary ruling from the ECJ on the matter and there was no genuine dispute.

Held The ECJ refused to give a preliminary ruling on the grounds that there was no real dispute.

Foglia v Novello (No 2) Case 244/80

Following the decision in the (No 1) case above, the Italian court sought a further preliminary ruling, asking what action it should take in the circumstances.

Held The ECJ declined again to give a ruling for the same reasons and stated that it had no jurisdiction to rule on hypothetical questions.

Note ─────────────────────────

In the interval between *Foglia (No 1)* and *Foglia (No 2)*, the cases of *Chemial v DAF* Case 140/79 and *Vinal v Orbat* Case 46/80 were heard. Both had almost exactly the same facts as *Foglia*, but the tax was an Italian tax – in both cases the reference was accepted by the ECJ.

Wienand Meilicke v ADV/ORGA FA Meyer AG Case C-83/91
The ECJ refused to give a ruling when it took the view that the German court had posed a hypothetical question, not relevant to the dispute.

Max Mara Case C-307/95
The Court refused to give a ruling on the grounds that the national court had provided an inadequate description of the facts and the relevant national law.

Dias (Lourenco) v Director de Alfandega do Porto Case C-343/90
The ECJ refused to give a preliminary ruling on the majority of questions referred to it because they had no connection with the dispute which the national court was called upon to resolve.

TWD Textilwerke Deggendorf GmbH v Bundesrepublik Deutschland Case 188/92
The Commission issued a Decision to Germany stating that the aid that the German authorities had granted to TWD, a textile company, was contrary to the Treaty and had to be repaid. The company was advised, by the German authorities, that it had the right to challenge the Commission Decision under Article 230 EC (ex 173). Since the company was expressly named in the Commission Decision, it would have been able to prove direct and individual concern.

However, TWD failed to bring an action within the prescribed time limits. The company then, at a later date, sought to challenge the validity of the Commission Decision in the course of proceedings before the national courts.

Held The Commission refused to give a preliminary ruling on the validity of the Decision (under Article 234 EC (ex 177)) on the grounds that the company clearly knew about its rights under Article 230 EC (ex 173) and had failed to take them up.

This ruling has been relaxed to some extent in the following case.

R v Intervention Board for Agriculture ex p Accrington Beef Co Ltd Case C-241/95

In this case the Accrington Beef Co Ltd had failed to bring a judicial review action under Article 230 EC (ex 173) (see Chapter 4) within the strict time limits. They sought to challenge an EC Regulation during a domestic judicial review action. Notwithstanding this, the ECJ accepted the request for a preliminary ruling. The Court recognised that the company was not clear that it would have had the necessary *locus standi* to bring such an action. (For a discussion of the *locus standi* of individuals in EC judicial review actions, see Chapter 4.)

5.9   The effect of a preliminary ruling

Milch-Fett und Eirkontor v HZA Saarbrücken Case 29/68

Held The ECJ held that a preliminary ruling given by the ECJ under Article 234 EC (ex 177) is binding upon the national court from which the reference was made.

5.10   Interim relief pending a preliminary ruling

R v Secretary of State for Transport ex p Factortame Ltd (No 1) Case C–213/89

A group of Spanish fishermen challenged the provisions of the Merchant Shipping Act 1988 alleging that the legislation contravened the principle of non-discrimination on the grounds of nationality contained in the Treaty (Article 12 EC (ex 6)) and infringed their right of establishment under Article 43 EC (ex 52). The fishermen had set up a UK company in order to obtain a UK fishing quota. The Merchant Shipping Act 1988 provided that a company must be owned by at least 75% UK nationals living in the UK. The question faced by the House of Lords was whether they could grant interim relief for the fishermen, pending a ruling from the ECJ on the substantive issues of the case.

Held The ECJ held that national courts are obliged to provide a sufficient remedy to protect rights derived under Community law. Where national law does not provide an adequate remedy, the court must provide one. In the case in point, the ECJ held that an interim injunction could be made against the Crown where there was no other means of protecting the individuals' rights under Community law.

Note ————————————————————————————————
For further discussion of the *Factortame* case, see 6.2.2.

Zuckerfabrik Süderdithmarschen AG v Hauptzollamt Itzehoe Cases C-143/88 and C-92/89

This action arose out of two separate disputes in Germany between companies and the German customs authorities regarding demands for the payment of levies. The companies challenged the German administrative measures on the grounds that they were based on invalid Community legislation. Following *Foto-Frost* (see above, 5.2.2), the German court could not rule on the validity of the Community Regulation and had to seek a preliminary ruling. The national court also raised the issue of whether the national court could grant interim relief against the contested measure.

Held The ECJ held that it is possible for a national court to grant interim relief, suspending the enforcement of a national measure, where the validity of the Community measure is contested. However, interim relief may only be provided where:

(1) the national court, in the light of the factual and legal circumstances, has serious doubts about the validity of the Community measure;

(2) suspension of a national measure can only be granted until such time as the ECJ rules on the validity of the Community measure; and

(3) interim relief may only be granted in the event of urgency, in order to avoid serious and irreparable damage to the party seeking relief.

6 Supremacy of Community Law

6.1 The supremacy of Community law as developed by the Court of Justice

6.1.1 The European Community constitutes a new legal order

NV Algemene Transport-en Expeditie Onderneming Van Gend en Loos v Nederlandse Administratie der Belastingen Case 26/62

Van Gend en Loos imported ureaformaldehyde from Germany into the Netherlands. The firm (VGL) was charged an 8% customs duty by the Dutch authorities. VGL complained that the chemicals should only have been subject to a 3% customs duty and that the levy of an 8% duty by the Dutch authorities was a breach of Article 25 EC (ex 12) which prohibited the introduction, by Member States, of new customs duties. The Dutch court sought a reference from the ECJ, asking whether VGL was entitled to rely on the provisions of Article 25 EC (ex 12).

Held It was held by the ECJ that:

> The conclusion to be drawn from this is that the Community constitutes a new legal order of international law for the benefit of which the States have limited their sovereign rights, albeit within limited fields, and the subjects of which comprise not only Member States but also their nationals.

The provisions of Article 25 EC (ex 12) were held to be directly effective and enforceable by VGL in the Dutch Courts. (For further discussion, see Chapter 7.)

6.1.2 Membership of the Community results in a limitation of sovereign rights

Costa v ENEL Case 6/64

C sought a declaration from the Italian court that he was not obliged to pay his electricity bill (less than £2!) on the grounds that the Italian law which had nationalised the electricity industry in 1962 and created the new company, ENEL, was contrary to certain provisions of the EEC Treaty, including Article 31 EC (ex 37). The Italian court sought a preliminary ruling on the relevant Community law provisions. However, the Italian Government intervened once the matter was referred to the ECJ and argued that the application for a preliminary ruling was wholly inadmissible because the dispute involved matters of national law unconnected with the Treaty.

Held The EEC Treaty had created a new legal order which was an integral element of the legal systems of the Member States. By creating a Community of unlimited duration with its own institutions, there had been a transfer of power from the Member States to the Community and the Member States had limited their sovereign rights. Member States cannot give preference to a unilateral and subsequent measure against a legal order accepted by them on the basis of reciprocity.

6.1.3 Community law prevails over a Member State's constitutional law

Internationale Handelgesellschaft GmbH v EVST Case 11/70

A German company obtained an export licence to export maize before 31 December 1967. Under a Council Regulation, the export licence deposit was to be forfeited if the export did not take place within the prescribed period. The company lost a part of its deposit when it did not export all the maize by the set date. The company challenged the deposit scheme and the German Court came to the view that the deposit scheme was contrary to certain principles enshrined in the German Constitution. A preliminary ruling was sought from the ECJ questioning the validity of the Council Regulation.

Held The validity of Community measures can only be judged in the light of Community law. The Court made it clear that 'the law stemming from the Treaty ... cannot because of its very nature be overridden by rules of national law, however framed'. To give priority to a national law, even that contained in a constitution, would undermine the legal basis of the Community.

6.2 Conflicting domestic law

Commission v Italy Case 168/85

In proceedings against Italy, the ECJ held that a Member State is under a duty to repeal any domestic legislation which is incompatible with the Treaty. The incompatibility of national legislation with provisions of the Treaty, even provisions which are directly effective, can be fully remedied only by means of national provisions of a binding nature which have the same legal force as those which must be amended.

6.2.1 A national court must set aside any conflicting national laws and give effect to Community law

Amministrazione delle Finanze dello Stato v Simmenthal SpA (No 2)
Case 106/77

S, an Italian company, imported meat from other Member States into Italy. As the meat crossed the border into Italy, it was subject to health inspections. The costs of the inspections were levied on the imported goods. S sought to recover the levy paid in the Italian courts. The ECJ gave a preliminary ruling stating that the Italian law was contrary to Article 28 EC (ex 30), so that the Italian court could make an order for recovery of the sums paid. The Italian authorities objected to the constitutionality of the order and argued that the Italian court could not make the order unless the offending national legislation was repealed by the legislature, or referred to the Italian Constitutional Court. The Italian court sought a further preliminary ruling, asking whether national measures which conflicted with Community law could be disregarded without waiting for their repeal.

Held The ECJ held that a national court is under a duty to give full effect to provisions of Community law. Therefore, a national court must, if necessary, refuse of its own motion to apply any conflicting provisions of national legislation, even where enacted subsequently. It is not necessary for the national court to wait for the national legislation to be repealed, nor is it necessary for the national court to wait for the decision of a higher national court.

6.2.2 A national court must set aside any rules preventing it from interim relief, if it would otherwise grant interim relief

R v Secretary of State for Transport ex p Factortame Ltd and Others (No 1)
Case C-213/89

Factortame Ltd, a company incorporated in the UK, whose directors and shareholders were largely Spanish nationals, owned and operated fishing vessels registered as British. In 1988, the Government enacted the Merchant Shipping Act. Under the Act, all fishing vessels had to be registered and, in order to register, 75% of the directors and shareholders had to be British. The purpose of the Act was essentially to prevent foreign vessels from using up the British fishing quota. Factortame and a number of other companies brought a judicial review action in the English High Court, challenging the new nationality rules and arguing that they were contrary to Community law. The applicants also sought interim relief pending a final decision in the case. The High Court granted interim relief, effectively setting aside the provisions of the Act, and sought a preliminary ruling on the substantive issue of the case (whether the rules were contrary to EC law). The issue of interim relief was appealed and eventually came before the House of Lords. The issue before the House of Lords was whether interim relief could be granted. The House of Lords decided that, under common law, the courts had no power to grant interim relief against the Crown and that no court could restrain the enforcement of an Act of Parliament. However, the House of Lords nevertheless sought a ruling from the ECJ on whether, in Community law, it was bound to grant such interim relief.

Held The ECJ held that any provisions of a national legal system which prevent a national court from setting aside national laws which might prevent, even temporarily, Community law from having full force, are incompatible with Community law. The ECJ held that a national court, which would otherwise grant interim relief, must set aside any national rule which prevents it from granting such relief.

Note ───

In *R v Secretary of State ex p Factortame and Others (No 1)* Case C-213/89, the House of Lords considered the ruling given by the ECJ regarding the granting of interim relief. Taking into account the following factors, the House of Lords granted interim relief:

- the balance of convenience;
- whether damages would be an adequate remedy;
- the importance of upholding the law;
- the strength of the case.

───

6.2.2 A national court must set aside any procedural rule which precludes giving effect to Community law

Van Campenhout and Cie SCS v Belgium Case C-312/93

VC appealed against a decision of a lower court in Belgium in a case concerning a tax on dividends. Before the Belgian Court of Appeal, the applicants raised a new plea, arguing that the tax was contrary to Article 43 EC (ex 52). However, under Belgian procedural law, the argument was inadmissible, because it amounted to a new plea outside the statutory time limit. There was no other procedural stage at which this plea could have been considered. The Belgian Court of Appeal sought a ruling on whether or not it should set aside the national procedural rule and consider the argument.

Held The ECJ held that it is contrary to Community law to apply a domestic procedural rule which precludes a national court from considering the compatibility of domestic law with Community law of its own motion.

Emmott v Minister for Social Welfare Case 208/90

E, an Irish national, married with two dependant children, argued that she was entitled to the same social security benefits as that paid to a man in an identical situation to hers, and that her entitlement ran from December 1994, the date by which Member States were required to implement the Social Security Directive (79/7/EEC). The implementing legislation in Ireland, the Social Welfare (No 2) Act 1995 made no provision for retrospective payment to December 1994. E sought judicial review in order to recover her benefits, but her action was struck out on the grounds that she had not brought her action within the prescribed time limits. The Irish High Court asked the ECJ whether Member States could rely on national procedural rules in these circumstances.

Held In proceedings by an individual before the national courts, the ECJ held that, in order to protect rights directly conferred by a Directive, Community law precludes the authorities from relying on national procedural rules relating to time limits for bringing proceedings against them. This applies in circumstances where the Member State has not properly transposed that Directive into its domestic legal system.

6.3   A national court must interpret national law to give full effect to Community law

Marleasing SA v La Comercial Internacional de Alimentacíon SA Case C-106/89

A Spanish company was formed, allegedly for the purpose of defrauding the creditors of the founding members. The creditors sought to have the company voided on the grounds of lack of consideration, or alternatively lack of lawful cause. The defendants argued that the only grounds for voiding a company were contained in Article 11 of Council Directive 68/151/EEC and that voiding the company formation on any other grounds would be contrary to the Directive. The Directive had not been implemented in Spanish law.

Held The ECJ made it clear that:

> ... in applying national law, whether the provisions in question were adopted *before or after* the Directive, the national court called upon to interpret it is required to do so, so far as possible, in the light of the wording and the purpose of the Directive in order to achieve the result pursued by the [Directive] ...

The Spanish court was required, so far as possible, to interpret Spanish legislation enacted before the Directive in the light of the Directive, in order to give it effect.

6.3.1   The response of the English courts

Re Westinghouse Uranium Contract (1978)

Lord Denning stated:

> The EEC Treaty and all its provisions are now part of the law of England: that is clear from s 2 of the European Communities Act 1972. We have to give force to the Treaty as being incorporated lock, stock and barrel into our own law here.

The rule of construction approach – s 2(4) of the European Communities Act 1972

Macarthys Ltd v Smith Case 129/79

This case involved a claim for equal pay brought by Smith against her employers. In the Court of Appeal, Denning LJ stated that the provisions of the Sex Discrimination Act 1970 should be construed to give effect to Article 141 EC (ex 119): 'in construing Acts of Parliament, the courts are entitled to "look to the Treaty as an aid to construction: and ... as an overriding force".' However, Denning LJ also made it clear that 'Unless there is an express intention by Parliament to repudiate the Treaty, the national courts should give priority to Community law'. Therefore, if Parliament expressly repudiates EC law the courts will give priority to domestic legislation.

Garland v British Rail Engineering Ltd Case 12/81

Mrs Garland complained against a British Rail rule which allowed the families of male ex-employees concessionary rail fares after retirement, but which did not allow the same privilege for families of female ex-employees. Under s 6(4) of the Sex Discrimination Act 1975, provisions relating to retirement were exempted from the sex discrimination rules. A preliminary ruling was sought asking whether Article 141 EC (ex 119) covered retirement and the ECJ held that it did.

Following the preliminary ruling from the ECJ, which had stated that the Sex Discrimination Act 1975 should be construed in the light of Article 141 EC (ex 119), the House of Lords (Lord Diplock) stated that, as a principle of construction, 'the words of a statute passed after the Treaty ... are to be construed, if they are reasonably capable of bearing such a meaning, as intended to carry the obligation [of the Treaty]'.

Held The House of Lords held that s 6(4) of the Sex Discrimination Act 1975 must be construed to conform with Article 141 EC (ex 119).

Pickstone v Freemans plc (1989)

The English Court of Appeal was faced with the interpretation of a 1983 statutory instrument, amending the Sex Discrimination Act 1970, which had been introduced to give effect to an EC Directive. The Court of Appeal found that the words of the statutory instrument were clear and unambiguous, but that Community law should prevail. (In other words, the Court of Appeal was happy to give priority to Community law.)

Held The House of Lords, however, held that a purposive interpretation should be given to the domestic legislation, even though this meant going against the literal meaning and reading certain words into the domestic law in order to achieve the aims of the Directive. The House of Lords justified this on the basis that the legislation was intended by Parliament to give effect to Community law.

Litster v Forth Dry Dock and Engineering Co Ltd (1989)

L and a number of other employees claimed unfair dismissal when their employer was taken over by another company. They sought to rely on the provisions of the Transfer of Undertakings (Protection of Employment) Regulations 1981 which were intended to implement Directive 77/187/EEC. The implementing Regulation contained a number of ambiguities.

The House of Lords interpreted the UK Regulation to comply with the Directive and, in doing so, applied the *Von Colson* principle (see Chapter 8). The Court indicated that, where legislation has been introduced to give effect to a Directive, the national courts must interpret the implementing legislation to give effect to the Directive, even if this required the court to supply 'the necessary words by implication'.

A national court can only construe domestic legislation to give effect to Community law if it is possible to do so

Webb v EMO Air Cargo (UK) Ltd Case C-32/93

In the House of Lords, Lord Keith stated that:

> ... a national court must construe a domestic law to accord with the terms of a Directive in the same field only if it is possible to do so. That means that the domestic law must be open to an interpretation consistent with the Directive whether or not it is also open to an interpretation inconsistent with it.

McKechnie v UBM Building Supplies (Southern) Ltd (1991)

M based a claim for redundancy pay on Article 141 EC (ex 119) of the Treaty since there was no domestic legislation supporting M's claim. The Employment Appeal Tribunal found in favour of M. Although there was no domestic law which could be construed in the light of Article 141 EC (ex 119) the Tribunal was willing to apply Article 141 EC (ex 119) directly.

7 Direct Effect of Community Law

7.1 Direct effect of Treaty provisions

NV Algemene Transport-en Expeditie Onderneming Van Gend en Loos v Nederlandse Administratie der Belastingen Case 26/62

Van Gend en Loos imported ureaformaldehyde from Germany into the Netherlands. The firm (VGL) was charged an 8% customs duty by the Dutch authorities. VGL complained that the chemicals should only have been subject to a 3% customs duty and that the levy of an 8% duty by the Dutch authorities was a breach of Article 25 EC (ex 12), which prohibited the introduction by Member States of new customs duties. The Dutch court sought a reference from the ECJ on whether VGL was entitled to rely on the provisions of Article 25 EC (ex 12).

Held The provisions of Article 25 EC (ex 12) are directly effective and create individual rights which national courts must protect. For a provision of Community law to be directly effective, it must satisfy the following conditions:

(1) it must be clear and precise;

(2) it must contain an unconditional prohibition; and

(3) it must not allow any discretion on the part of Member States in the implementation:

> The conclusion to be drawn from this is that the Community constitutes a new legal order of international law for the benefit of which the States have limited their sovereign rights, albeit within limited fields, and the subjects of which comprise not only Member States but also their nationals. Independently of the legislation of Member States, Community law therefore not only imposes obligations on individuals but is also intended to confer upon them rights which become part of their legal heritage. These rights arise not only when they are expressly granted by the Treaty, but also by reason of the obligations which the Treaty imposes in a clearly defined way upon individuals as well as upon Member States and upon the institutions of the Community.

Costa v ENEL Case 6/64

C sought a declaration from the Italian court that he was not obliged to pay his electricity bill (less than £2!) on the grounds that the Italian law which had nationalised the electricity industry in 1962 and which had created the new company, ENEL, was contrary to certain provisions of the EEC Treaty, including Article 31 EC (ex 37) (see, also, Chapter 6).

Held Article 31 EC (ex 37) contains an absolute prohibition, capable of producing direct effects on the legal relations between Member States and their nationals:

> Such a clearly expressed prohibition ... became an integral part of the legal systems of the Member States, forms part of the law of those States, and directly concerns their nationals, in whose favour it creates individual rights which the national courts must protect.

7.1.1 Provisions containing positive obligations may also be directly effective

Lütticke (Alfons) GmbH v Hauptzollamt Saarlouis Case 57/65

The German customs authorities demanded a turnover equalisation tax payable on the import of a consignment of milk powder from Luxembourg into Germany. Lütticke appealed to the German customs court against the tax. He based his argument on Article 90(1) EC (ex 95(1)) which prohibits the imposition of discriminatory internal taxes and Article 90(3) EC (ex 95(3)) which places a positive obligation on Member States to repeal or amend any national laws which are contrary to Article 90(1) EC (ex 95(1)). The German customs court sought a preliminary ruling from the ECJ asking whether Article 90(3) EC (ex 95(3)), containing a positive obligation, as opposed to a prohibition (as in *NV Algemene Transport-en Expeditie Onderneming Van Gend en Loos v Nederlands Administratie der Belastingen*), could have direct effect.

Held Article 90(3) EC (ex 95(3)) contained a general rule which imposes a clear and unconditional obligation on Member States to refrain from measures introducing discriminatory internal taxation. Article 90(3) EC (ex 95(3)) was therefore held to be directly effective. Direct effect is not confined to prohibitory measures.

7.2 Horizontal direct effect of Treaty Articles

Defrenne (Gabrielle) v Société Anonyme Belge de Navigation Aérienne SABENA (No 2) Case 43/75

D worked for SABENA Airlines as a stewardess. She received less pay than the male stewards who were doing the same work. D brought a claim for equal pay in the Belgian courts and sought to rely on the provisions of

Article 141 EC (ex 119) of the EEC Treaty ('Member States shall ... ensure and maintain the principle that men and women should receive equal pay for equal work'). The Belgian court sought a preliminary ruling from the ECJ – could Article 141 EC (ex 119) (a positive obligation on Member States) be relied upon by individuals in the national courts?

Held Since Article 141 EC (ex 119) is mandatory in nature, the prohibition on discrimination between men and women applies not only to the action between public authorities but also extends to all agreements which are intended to regulate paid labour collectively, as well as contracts between individuals. Article 141 EC (ex 119) is directly effective and therefore conferred a legal right upon D, enforceable in the national courts, *and* a legal obligation upon SABENA. (This is known as horizontal direct effect.)

BRT v SABAM (No 1) Case 127/73

Held Articles 81 and 82 EC (ex 85 and 86), by their very nature, produce direct effects in relations between individuals. Consequently, these Articles create rights which must be safeguarded by national courts.

7.3 National courts must set aside any provisions of national law which may conflict with directly effective Community law

Amministrazione delle Finanze dello Stato v Simmenthal SpA (No 2) Case 106/77

Following a preliminary ruling from the ECJ to the effect that fees charged for veterinary inspections were contrary to Article 25 EC (ex 12) of the EEC Treaty and the inspection contrary to Article 28 EC (ex 30), the Italian court ordered the Italian Finance Ministry to repay to S the fees charged. The Treaty Articles were held to be directly effective and enforceable by S in the Italian courts. The Ministry argued that they could not repay the fees as they were bound, under the Italian constitution, to the national statute until such time as the national law was set aside by the Italian constitutional court.

Held The ECJ, giving a preliminary ruling, held that every national court must apply Community law in its entirety and protect rights conferred on individuals. The court must accordingly set aside any provision of national law which may conflict with directly effective Community law, whether the national law was passed prior or subsequent to the Community rule. (See Chapter 6 for further discussion of this case.)

7.4 Direct effect of EC secondary legislation

7.4.1 Regulations

Leonesio v Italian Ministry of Agriculture (Re Slaughtered Cow) Case 93/71
Held The ECJ held that any rights conferred by an EC Regulation cannot be subjected to any national implementing measures.

Fratelli Variola SpA v Amministrazione Italiana delle Finanze Case 34/73
A preliminary ruling was sought as to whether the provisions of a Regulation could be implemented by domestic measures which effectively reproduced the provisions of the Regulation.

Held Again, the ECJ held that the direct application of a Regulation means that its entry into force and its application in favour of those subject to it are independent of any implementing measures.

Taittinger v Allbev Ltd (1993)
The Court of Appeal in England held that Article 15(5) of Regulation (EEC) 832/87 was directly effective and could be enforced by an aggrieved party against another person.

7.4.2 Decisions

Franz Grad v Finanzamt Traunstein Case 9/70
A German company challenged a tax imposed by the German Government. The company argued that the tax contravened Directive 67/227/EEC, requiring Member States to amend their VAT systems and Council Decision 65/271/EEC, which set out the time periods for implementation of the Directive. A preliminary ruling was sought from a German court on whether Article 4 of Decision 65/271/EEC, in conjunction with Article 1 of Directive 67/227/EEC, could be directly effective against the State and thus create rights for the company which the national court must protect.

Held Although Regulations are, by virtue of Article 249 EC (ex 189), directly applicable, it does not follow that other secondary legislation measures referred to in Article 249 (ex 189) cannot produce direct effect. It would be incompatible with the binding effect attributed to Decisions to exclude the possibility of their direct effect. The ECJ stated that, in each particular case, it must be determined whether the nature, background and wording of the provision in question are capable of producing direct effects in the legal relationship between the addressee of the act and third parties.

Note ───
The Court did not specifically deal with the issue of the direct effect of Directives, but it did not rule out the possibility.

7.5 Direct effect of Directives

Van Duyn v Home Office Case 41/74

VD was refused entry into the UK where she was due to take up employment with the Church of Scientology. This refusal was contrary to Article 39 EC (ex 48) of the Treaty on the freedom of movement of workers. The UK, however, sought to rely on one of the exceptions to Article 39 EC (ex 48), namely, that the refusal was justified on the grounds of public policy. Directive 64/221/EEC lays down provisions on the use of the public policy exception and VD sought to rely on the terms of the Directive.

Held ECJ held that Article 39 EC (ex 48) was directly effective. With regard to the Directive it held that it would be incompatible with the binding effect attributed to a Directive to exclude, in principle, the possibility that it may be invoked by an individual. The useful effect of a Directive would be weakened if individuals were prevented from relying on it before their national courts. However, it is necessary to examine, in every case, whether the nature, general scheme and wording of the provision in question are capable of direct effect. The relevant provisions of Directive 64/221/EEC were found to confer on individuals' rights which are enforceable in the courts of the Member States and which the national courts must protect. However, on the facts, the UK was entitled to refuse entry to VD (see Chapter 13).

7.5.1 Directives only capable of direct effect after period for implementation has expired

Pubblico Ministero v Tullio Ratti Case 148/78

R complied with the provisions of two Directives on the labelling of dangerous substances; in one case, in compliance with a Directive that Italy had failed to implement and, in the other, in anticipation of the provisions being implemented into Italian law, that is, before the date of implementation required by the Directive. R was charged with criminal offences because he had not complied with the (stricter) Italian law. R argued, in his defence, that the Italian courts should apply the provisions of the Directives, not the provisions of the Italian law.

Held The ECJ held that a Member State which has not adopted the implementing measures required by a Directive in the prescribed period may not rely, against individuals such as R, on its own failure to perform the obligations under the Directive. Therefore, after the period within which a Directive must be implemented, a Member State may not apply its internal law to a person who has complied with the Directive. R could rely on the direct effect of the unimplemented Directive. However, it is only after the deadline for implementation that a Directive will become directly effective; before that date, the existing domestic law prevails.

Note ─────────
This is a good example of EC law being invoked as a defence to a criminal charge.

Becker v Finanzamt Münster-Innenstadt Case 8/81

B sought certain tax exemptions which were calculated in accordance with a Council Directive on the harmonisation of turnover taxes. The deadline for the implementation of the Directive had passed and Germany had failed to implement the Directive. However, the German authorities argued against the direct effect of the Directive, on the grounds that it gave the Member States a degree of discretion with regard to tax exemptions and that, since certain provisions of the Directive would be unfavourable to certain individuals, they could not have effect until such time as the Member State had clearly implemented them.

Held The ECJ stated that, whilst the Directive confers varying degrees of discretion on Member States, individuals must not be denied the right to rely on any provisions of the Directive which are capable of being 'severed from the general body of provisions and applied separately'. The court took a very flexible position regarding the requirement of absence of discretion needed for direct effect. The Court was clear that a Member State which has not adopted a Directive on time cannot argue against an individual that it has not fulfilled the obligations arising from the Directive.

Verbond Van Nederlandse Ondernemingen v Inspecteur der Invoerrechten en Accijnzen Case 51/76

The Federation of Dutch Manufacturers sought to rely directly on the provisions of the second VAT Directive to support their case even though the Directive had been implemented into Dutch law.

Held The ECJ held that a Directive may be invoked after implementation to allow individuals access to the courts to determine whether the implementing authorities have acted within their powers.

7.5.2 National authorities cannot rely on the direct effect of an unimplemented directive against an individual

Officier Van Justitie v Kolpinghuis Nijmegen BV Case 80/86

KN was prosecuted for stocking mineral water which contained additives contrary to Directive 80/777/EEC. However, the Dutch Government had not in fact implemented the Directive.

Held The ECJ held that the Dutch authorities could not rely on the direct effect of an unimplemented Directive against an individual. A State cannot plead, as against an individual, its own failure to implement a Directive. See, also, *Becker v Finanzamt Münster-Innenstadt* (1981), above, 7.5.1.

7.5.3 Directives are only directly effective against the state or an emanation of the state – no horizontal direct effect

Marshall v Southampton and South West Area Health Authority (Teaching) (No 1) Case 152/84

M, who worked for the area health authority, wished to retire at the age of 65. However, the policy of the authority was that women should retire at 60 and men at 65. M was dismissed at the age of 62 and took the area health authority to the industrial tribunal, claiming this was unlawful discrimination contrary to the Equal Treatment Directive (76/207/EEC) (the Directive had not been properly implemented by the UK). On appeal, the Court of Appeal sought a preliminary ruling from the ECJ as to whether M could rely on the Directive. The area health authority argued that, although a Directive may have direct effect against the State (as in *Van Gend en Loos v Nederlandse Administratie der Belastingen* Case 26/62 – see above, 7.1), a Directive can never impose obligations directly on individuals, and could not, therefore, be directly effective against the area health authority (as an employer).

Held The ECJ held that 'It follows [in the light of the wording of Article 189 (now 249 EC)] that a Directive may not, of itself, impose obligations on an individual and that the provision of a Directive may not be relied upon as such against such a person'. In other words, Directives are only capable of vertical direct effect. They cannot be horizontally directly effective. However, the ECJ held that the area health authority was part of the State for these purposes.

Where a person is able to rely on a Directive against the State they can do so whether the State is acting as an employer or public authority, hence, M could rely on the provisions of the Directive.

Note ───

The consistent theme in these cases is that it is necessary to prevent the State taking advantage of its own failure to comply with Community law.

───

Faccini Dori v Recreb Srl Case C-91/92

FD sought to rely on the provisions of a Directive in order to cancel a contract for a language course. Under the provisions of the Directive, contracts made away from business premises (as in the case in hand) were subject to a seven day period during which time the contract could be cancelled. The Directive had not been implemented in Italy.

Held The ECJ held that the Directive, although sufficiently clear and precise, could not give rise to horizontal direct effect. In doing so it confirmed its Decision in *Marshall v Southampton and South West Area Health Authority (Teaching) (No 1)* Case 152/84.

Note

Although the ECJ denied the horizontal direct effect of Directives, the Court made the point that alternative remedies might be available to individuals. These alternative remedies, indirect effect and state liability, are discussed in the following chapter.

7.6　What constitutes the State or an emanation of the State?

Local and regional authorities

Fratelli Costanzo SpA v Commune di Milano Case 103/88

C brought an action against the Municipality of Milan, arguing that its public works contract procedures (in preparation for the 1990 Football World Cup in Italy) were contrary to a Council Directive on public works procurement. The Italian court sought a preliminary ruling, asking whether the municipality was bound by the Directive.

Held The ECJ held that 'all organs of administration, including decentralised authorities such as municipalities, are obliged to apply [these] provisions'.

R v London Boroughs Transport Committee ex p Freight Association Ltd (1991)

Held The English High Court held that a local authority is an organ of the State.

Johnston v Chief Constable of the Royal Ulster Constabulary Case 222/84

Johnston sought to rely on Directive 76/207/EEC to challenge the RUC Chief Constable's rules that men should carry firearms but women should not, and that women should not be assigned to general police duties. J's contract was not renewed in line with this policy.

Held An authority such as the Chief Constable is an official responsible for the direction of the police service and, as such, is part of the State. Accordingly, J could rely on the provisions of the Directive against the Chief Constable.

Foster v British Gas plc Case C-188/89

F and others were employed by British Gas. They were forced to retire at the age of 60 in line with company policy (five years before male employees). The women wished to continue working, sought damages from British Gas and argued that their retirement was contrary to Article 5(1) of Directive 76/207/EEC. The House of Lords sought a preliminary ruling on whether the terms of the directive could be relied upon against British Gas, that is, whether British Gas plc could be considered an emanation of the State. At the time of the action, British Gas was a nationalised industry.

Held The ECJ, on a reference from the House of Lords, held that a body, whatever its legal form, which has been made responsible by the State for providing a public service under the control of the State, and has, for that purpose, special powers beyond those normally applicable between individuals, is an emanation of the State.

Doughty v Rolls Royce plc (1992)

In this case, the facts were very similar to *Foster v British Gas*. D, who worked for Rolls Royce plc, was forced to retire at the age of 60 in line with the company's retirement policy. She sought to rely on the provisions of Directive 75/207/EEC, which had not been properly implemented by the UK. The case was not referred to the ECJ.

Held The Court of Appeal held that Rolls Royce was not an emanation of the State. Although it was nationalised, it had not been made responsible by the State for providing a public service. Thus, the Court of Appeal placed a restrictive interpretation on the ECJ's ruling in *Foster*.

Unison v South West Water (1994)

The trade union Unison sought to rely on the provisions of a Directive against the employers South West Water.

Held Blackburn LJ (Court of Appeal) held that South West Water was an emanation of the State because the company was 'a State authority.' The relevant question is not whether the *body* in question is under the control of the State, but whether the *public service* in question is under the control of the State. The fact that the overall control of water services is exercised by the State was the relevant factor, not the legal form of the body, nor the fact that the body was a commercial concern.

National Union of Teachers v Governing Body of Saint Mary's Church of England (Aided) Junior School (1997)

In this case, the Court of Appeal held that the concept of the emanation of the State should be given a broad interpretation . The Court of Appeal held that the definition of an emanation of the State provided by the ECJ in *Foster* should not be the exhaustive statutory definition. In this case, the governing body of a voluntary aided school was held to be an emanation of the State.

8 Extending the Effect of Community Law – the Duty of Interpretation and State Liability

8.1 The duty of interpretation

Von Colson and Kamann v Land Nordrhein-Westfalen Case 14/83 and Harz v Deutsche Tradax GmbH Case 79/83

VC was rejected when she applied to work in the prison service and H was rejected when she applied to work in a private company. They both brought actions in the German courts on the grounds that their rejection was based on their sex. The German court found in their favour, but limited the award of damages to their travelling expenses to and from the interviews. Both women argued that these damages contravened the Equal Treatment Directive 76/207/EEC, which requires Member States to enable persons claiming a breach of the equality principle to pursue their claims through the judicial process. H was seeking to enforce the provisions of the Directive against a private company and not the State.

Held The ECJ held that the relevant provisions of the Directive were not sufficiently precise or unconditional for the Directive to be directly effective. Instead, the Court provided an alternative remedy which is known as indirect effect or the 'obligation of interpretation'. The Court held that a Member State has an obligation to achieve the results prescribed in a Directive (Article 249 EC (ex 189)) and Article 10 EC (ex 5) requires them to take all appropriate measures, whether general or particular, to ensure the fulfilment of their obligation. This obligation is binding on all authorities of the Member States, including the national courts. Thus, the national courts are under a duty to interpret national law in such a manner as to ensure that the objectives of the Directive are achieved. In this case, the German courts were required to interpret the German law in such a way as to provide an adequate judicial remedy, as was required by Article 6 of the Directive.

Officier van Justitie v Kolpinghuis Nijmegen Case 80/86

Criminal charges were brought against KN, for selling bottles of carbonated tap water as mineral water. The prosecution sought, amongst other things, to rely on the provisions of a 1980 Directive which had not yet been implemented into Dutch law. The Dutch court sought a preliminary ruling from the ECJ, asking whether the provisions of an unimplemented Directive could be enforced by the State against an individual and whether the national court is under a duty to interpret domestic law in the light of the unimplemented Directive.

Held The ECJ held that a national authority may not rely, as against an individual, upon a provision of a Directive whose necessary implementation in national law has not yet taken place. (A Member State cannot benefit from its own failure to fulfil Community law obligations.) On the question of interpretation, the Court ruled that the obligation to interpret the relevant national law in the light of a Directive is limited by the principles of legal certainty and non-retroactivity. (See Chapter 9 for further discussion.) A Directive cannot of itself, and independently of national implementing legislation, have the effect of determining or aggravating the liability of criminal law of persons who breach the provisions of the Directive.

8.1.1   *Marleasing* – extending the duty of interpretation

Marleasing SA v La Comercial Internacional de Alimentacion SA Case C-106/89

A Spanish company was formed, allegedly for the purpose of defrauding the creditors of the founding members. The creditors sought to have the company voided on the grounds of lack of consideration or, alternatively, lack of lawful cause. The defendants argued that the only grounds for voiding a company were contained in Article 11 of Council Directive 68/151/EEC and that voiding the company formation on any other grounds would be contrary to the Directive. The Directive had not been implemented into Spanish law.

Held The Directive was not capable of producing direct effect between individuals (see *Marshall*, above, 7.5.3). However, the ECJ held that:

> It follows that, in applying national law, whether the provisions in question were adopted before or after the Directive, the national court called upon to interpret it is required to do so, so far as possible, in the light of the wording and the purpose of the Directive in order to achieve the result pursued by the [Directive] …

The Spanish court was required to interpret Spanish legislation (so far as possible) enacted before the Directive in order to give effect to the Directive.

The duty of interpretation applies whether or not the national legislation was adopted to implement a Community provision and applies in respect of national legislation which was passed before the Community provision.

The obligation of interpretation is limited by the general principles of Community law

Wagner Miret v Fondo de Garantía Salaria Case C-334/92

WM was a senior manager in a Spanish company which had gone into insolvency. He sought to rely on Directive 80/987/EEC which required Member States to implement a scheme which would reimburse employees wages in the event of their employers becoming insolvent. The Spanish Government had implemented the Directive, but had excluded senior managers from the scheme. The Spanish court sought a preliminary ruling, asking whether senior managers were covered by the Directive and, if they were, whether they were entitled to recover damages from the State for failing to provide for them.

Held The ECJ stated that, in interpreting national law to conform with the objectives of a Directive, the national court must assume that the national legislature intended to comply with Community law. The ECJ held that national courts must try 'as far as possible' to interpret domestic law to achieve the objectives of the Directive. However, the ECJ also made the point that if a national court cannot do this, the plaintiff may still be able to bring an action against the State for damages on the basis of the principle of state liability. (For a discussion of state liability, see below, 8.3).

Luciano Arcaro Case C-168/95

Held The obligation of interpretation is limited by the general principles of Community law, in particular, the principles of non-retroactivity and legal certainty (see Chapter 9 for further discussion). The ECJ held that the provisions of a Directive which has not been implemented cannot result in, or affect, the criminal liability of individuals who have acted in contravention to the Directive's provisions.

8.2   The reaction of the English courts to the duty of interpretation

Duke v GEC Reliance Ltd (1988)

Duke was forced by her employers, GEC, to retire at 60. The retirement age for male employees was 65. (Note the similarity of facts with *Marshall v Southampton Area Health Authority (Teaching)* (1986), see above, 7.5.3.) Unlike the *Marshall* case, the applicant could not rely on the directly effective provisions of Directive 76/207/EEC, because her action was against a private company and not against the State. Consequently, the House of Lords was asked to interpret s 6(4) of the Sex Discrimination Act 1975 in a way that would comply with the Directive.

Held The House of Lords limited the duty of interpretation to those provisions which were directly effective and accordingly were unwilling to construe the statute in the light of the Directive. The House of Lords ruled against D.

Note ───

Contrast this with the next case, which was also considered by the House of Lords.

Litster v Forth Dry Dock and Engineering Co Ltd (1989)

L and a number of other employees working for Forth Dry Dock Co (a private company) claimed unfair dismissal when their employer was taken over by another company. The plaintiffs sought to rely on the provisions of the Transfer of Undertakings (Protection of Employment) Regulations 1981, which were introduced to implement Directive 77/187/EEC. The implementing Regulations contained a number of ambiguities.

Held The House of Lords interpreted the UK Regulations in a way which complied with the Directive (and which was contrary to the *prima facie* meaning of the Regulations). Thus, the House of Lords applied the *Von Colson* principle.

Pickstone v Freemans plc (1989)

The English Court of Appeal was faced with the interpretation of a statutory instrument which had been introduced to give effect to an EEC Directive. The Court of Appeal found that the words of the statutory instrument were clear and unambiguous, but that Community law should prevail. The House of Lords held that a purposive interpretation should be given, even though this meant going against the literal meaning and reading certain words into the domestic legislation in order to achieve the aims of the Directive.

Webb v EMO Air Cargo UK Ltd Case C-32/93

In this case, W was temporarily employed to cover another employee who was on maternity leave. W was dismissed when she also became pregnant. W asserted that her dismissal was contrary to the Sex Discrimination Act 1975 and also Directive 76/207/EEC. The House of Lords held that the dismissal was not contrary to the Sex Discrimination Act 1975, but sought a ruling as to whether the dismissal was contrary to the Directive.

In the House of Lords, Lord Keith stated that a 'national court must construe a domestic law to accord with the terms of a Directive in the same field only if it is possible to do so. That means that the domestic law must be open to an interpretation consistent with the Directive, whether or not it is also open to an interpretation inconsistent with it'.

The House of Lords interpreted the Sex Discrimination Act 1975 in order to give effect to the interpretation of the Directive, as given by the ECJ in the preliminary ruling. Thus, it was held that W's dismissal was in breach of the Sex Discrimination Act 1975.

8.3 State liability for failure to fulfil obligations

Francovich and Bonifaci and Others v Republic of Italy Cases C-6/90 and C-9/90

F and others were owed wages from their employer following the employers insolvency. Under Council Directive 80/987/EEC, Member States were required to establish systems to guarantee such payments to employees in the event of employers' insolvency. The Italian Government had not implemented the Directive and no such guarantee scheme existed. F brought an action against the Italian State claiming the amounts they were owed.

Held The Directive in question was not sufficiently precise to be capable of direct effect. However, in this leading case, the ECJ went on to state that the State may be liable in damages in respect of harm caused to individuals by breaches of Community law, provided the following conditions could be satisfied:

(1) the Directive in question is capable of conferring rights on individuals and it should be possible to identify the contents of those rights; and

(2) the existence of a causal link between the breach of the State's obligation and the loss and damage suffered by the injured parties.

Brasserie du Pêcheur SA v Germany and R v Secretary of State for Transport ex p Factortame and Others (No 3) Joined Cases C-46 and 48/93

In Case C-46, B, a French company, claimed damages from the German Government, on the grounds that it was forced to discontinue beer exports into Germany between 1981 and 1989, because its beer did not conform to the German purity requirements. However the German law was found subsequently to be in breach of Article 28 EC (ex 30) (see *Commission v Germany* Case 78/84). In the *Factortame* case, F and others were claiming damages from the Department of Transport on the grounds that they had been deprived of their right to fish by the Merchant Shipping Act 1988, which was also held to be in breach of Community law. Unlike the *Francovich* case (see above), the domestic law was in breach of Treaty obligations rather than a failure to implement a Directive.

Held The claimants were entitled to seek damages in respect of the breaches of Community law where the national legislatures were responsible for the infringements. The ECJ went on to consider the conditions under which a Member State may incur liability and held that Community law confers a right to claim damages where three conditions are met:

(1) the rule of law infringed must be intended to confer rights on individuals;

(2) the breach must be sufficiently serious;

(3) there must be a direct causal link between the breach of the obligation on the Member State and the damage sustained by the injured party.

Thus, the conditions under which state liability gives a right to reparation depend upon the nature of the breach.

Note ──────────────────────────────────

The Court held that the conditions for state liability outlined above, must be similar to those laid down in Article 288 EC (ex 215) of the Treaty which lays down the liability of the Community institutions for breaches of Community law.

What constitutes a sufficiently serious breach of Community law?

In *Brasserie du Pecheur SA v Germany and Factortame (No 3)*, the ECJ held that a breach of Community law would be sufficiently serious where a Member State manifestly and gravely disregarded the limits of its discretion. The Court also identified certain factors which should be taken into account in determining whether a Member State had done this. These were:

* the extent of the Member State's discretion;

* the clarity of the rule of Community law breached by the Member State;

* whether the breach was intentional or not and whether the mistake was excusable or inexcusable.

The following cases consider these various factors.

R v HM Treasury ex p British Telecommunications plc Case C-392/93

This case concerned the implementation of Directive 90/531/EEC in the UK. A preliminary ruling was sought as to to whether the Directive had been implemented correctly, and, in the event that it had not, whether the State was liable in damages.

Held The ECJ held that a restrictive approach to State liability should be adopted in this case, because provisions of the Directive were ambiguous and the UK had acted in good faith when it had placed a particular interpretation on the Directive. Moreover, there was no guidance, in the form of case law from the ECJ, to guide the UK and the Commission had not raised any objections when the UK had advised it about the implementing legislation. Hence, the UK was held not to be liable in damages.

Denkavit International BV and VITAC Amsterdam BV and Voormeer BV v Bundesamt für Finanzamt Cases 283, 291 and 292/94

The ECJ reached a similar finding in respect of the German implementation of a Directive which was neither clear nor precise. In fact, most of the other Member States had incorrectly implemented the Directive in question.

R v Ministry of Agriculture, Fisheries and Food ex p Hedley Lomas (Ireland) Ltd Case C-5/94

For the facts, see below, 12.9.

In this case concerning the UK's breach of Article 29 EC (ex 34), the ECJ was asked to consider the award of damages.

Held First, the ECJ held that Article 29 EC (ex 34), while imposing a prohibition on Member States, also created rights for individuals which the national courts had to protect. The breach of Article 29 EC (ex 34) was sufficiently serious because, at the time, the State was not called on to make any legislative choices and had no discretion in the matter; the mere infringement of EC law, in such circumstances, could be sufficient to establish the existence of a serious breach. The fact that the Ministry had no proof of non-compliance by the Spanish slaughterhouse in question suggested a serious breach of EC law. The final condition, the requirement of a causal connection between the breach and damage was a matter for the national court to determine.

R v Secretary of State for the Home Department ex p Gallagher (1996)

G was seeking damages in respect of an alleged breach of Community law. G argued that the UK had, in enacting the Prevention of Terrorism (Temporary Provisions) Act 1989, incorrectly implemented an EC Directive.

On the facts, the English Court of Appeal decided that the breach was not sufficiently serious. Although the UK had exercised a degree of discretion and had made the wrong choice, its error was not (as in *Hedley Lomas*, above) a blatant breach. Also, the plaintiff, G, was 'not obviously worse off as a result' of the breach. (In other words, G did not establish a causal link between the breach and his losses.)

Dillenkofer and Others v Germany Cases C-179–87/94 and C-188–90/94

D, and various other would be tourists, had paid for a holiday with a package tour operator. D was forced to cancel the holiday when he became ill. He was unable to claim reimbursement of his money after the travel operator went into liquidation. He claimed damages against the German State, on the grounds that, had Germany implemented Directive 90/314/EEC on Package Holidays, within the prescribed period, he would have had a right to a refund.

Held The ECJ held that, where a Member State fails to implement a Directive within the period laid down, this will amount to a manifest and grave disregard to the limits of its discretion. The ECJ also held that the right to damages is not dependant upon a prior finding by the ECJ of an infringement of Community law.

Note ───────────────────────────────────

The Court referred back to its judgment in *Francovich* (see above) and stated that, whilst it had not 'expressly stated that there should be a sufficiently serious breach' of Community law, it was 'nevertheless evident from the circumstances of the case'. Thus, a failure to implement a Directive will amount to a sufficiently serious breach of Community law.

9 General Principles of Community Law

9.1 General principles drawn from the constitutional traditions of the Member States

Nold KG v Commission Case 4/73

N, a German coal wholesale company, challenged a Commission Decision under the ECSC Treaty. The Decision made it impossible for N to purchase coal from his supplier, because he could not fulfil the prescribed minimum purchase requirements. N claimed that the Decision, by depriving the company of direct supplies, violated its right to the free development of economic activity.

Held There was no such breach because the case was concerned with commercial interests. However, the Court went on the develop its position regarding the development of general principles. The Court draws its inspiration from the constitutional traditions common to the Member States and cannot, therefore, uphold measures which are incompatible with fundamental rights recognised and protected by the constitutions of those States.

General principles need not be common to all Member States

Hoogovens v High Authority Case 14/61

In the opinion of Advocate General Lagrange, 'The Court ... is not content to draw on more or less arithmetical "common denominators" between different national solutions, but chooses, from each of the Member States, those solutions which, having regard to the objects of the Treaty, appear to be the best ... the most progressive'.

Society for the Protection of Unborn Children v Grogan Case 159/90

In Ireland, abortions were forbidden, and thousands of women wanting an abortion were forced to travel to other Member States. The SPUC obtained an injunction from the Irish High Court in order to prevent a student's union in Dublin from distributing information about abortion services in other Member States. The information was found to contravene provisions in the Irish Constitution which upheld the right to life of the unborn child.

Held The ECJ held that the case did not involve an infringement of the right to provide services (see Chapter 14). However, Advocate General Van Gerven stated that there was a need to balance two fundamental rights – the right to life, as defined by one Member State, and the right to freedom of expression 'which is one of the principles of Community law'. The Court failed to take on board this balancing act, but in its judgment clearly protected a fundamental right of the particular Member State in question.

9.2 General principles drawn from international treaties

Nold KG v Commission Case 4/73

For facts, see above, 9.1.

Held The Court also held that, in addition to drawing upon the constitutional traditions of the Member States, international treaties for the protection of human rights, on which Member States have collaborated or which they have signed, can 'supply guidelines which should be followed within the framework of Community law'.

The European Convention of Human Rights may be invoked in the context of a case involving Community law

R v Kent Kirk Case 63/83

K, the captain of a Danish fishing boat, was charged and fined with fishing in British waters, contrary to a 1982 order. A subsequent EC Council regulation retroactively authorised the provisions of the UK law. K argued that the retroactive effect of the Council regulation was not justified because it could not retroactively validate penal provisions.

Held The ECJ, on a referral from the Crown Court, held that the principal of non-retroactivity of penal liability, as enshrined in Article 7 of the ECHR, could not be violated. The Court stated that a national measure in the sphere of Community law which breaches this right would be invalid.

Prais v Council Case 130/75

P applied for a post as an EC official and was required to take a competitive examination on a day that coincided with a Jewish festival. Observing the festival meant that P could not travel or write. P challenged the Commission Decision to hold the exam on that day and relied specifically on Article 9 of ECHR concerning freedom of religion.

Held The ECJ held that, since the Commission had not been told in advance by P of her religion, there was no religious discrimination. However, the Court said that, where advance information is provided, the

Commission should try to avoid dates which conflict with religious festivals.

Kaur v Lord Advocate (1980)

S, an Indian, challenged a deportation order made by the Scottish authorities under the terms of the Immigration Act 1971. He sought to rely on Article 8 of the ECHR (respect for family life).

Held K was not able to rely on the provisions of the Convention since it had not been incorporated into UK law. K could not invoke the provisions indirectly, via the European Communities Act 1972, in a matter which was completely unrelated to Community law.

Elliniki Radiophonia Tileorassi AE v Dimotiki Etairia Pliroforissis and Sotirios Kouvelas Case C-260/89

ERT, a Greek radio and television company, sought an injunction against DEP and SK to prevent the defendant's television station from broadcasting. ERT enjoyed an exclusive right to broadcast granted by statute. The defendants argued, *inter alia*, that this was a breach of the free movement of goods and ECHR relating to freedom of expression.

Held The Court held that where the matter falls under Community law, in this case, the freedom to provide services, any exceptions to that freedom must be appraised in the light of the general principle of freedom of expression, as embodied in Article 10 of the ECHR.

9.3   Fundamental rights

Stauder v City of Ulm Case 29/69

This case involved a Commission Decision to allow Member States to provide cheap butter for people on welfare benefits. Under Article 4 of the Decision, the butter could be provided in exchange for a coupon. S, a German, objected to the fact that he had to provide his name and address on the coupon in order to get the butter. He challenged this on the grounds that the requirement violated his human rights under the German Constitution. A preliminary ruling was sought from the German court asking whether the EC Decision creating the scheme was valid.

Held The ECJ held that the proper interpretation of the scheme did not require the applicant to supply his name and address on the coupon. The Court went on to say that the provisions at issue did nothing to prejudice 'the fundamental human rights enshrined in the general principle of Community law' and that such rights were to be protected by the Court.

Note ———

This was the first statement by the ECJ concerning the development of the principle of fundamental rights.

Internationale Handelsgesellschaft mbH v EVST Case 11/70

Exports of certain products were only permitted under the Common Agricultural Policy if the exporter had first obtained an export licence and paid a deposit. The deposit would be forfeited if the export was not carried out within the period of the licence. The applicants forfeited a part of their deposit when the licence expired without all the maize having been exported. The company claimed the return of the deposit and questioned the validity of the deposit.

Held The scheme did not infringe fundamental rights. Although the Court stated clearly that Community law would prevail over national law, including any fundamental rights provisions in a Member State's constitution, it also stated that it was necessary to examine Community law for equivalent principles. The Court held in relation to the development of fundamental rights that:

> ... respect for fundamental rights forms an integral part of the general principles of law protected by the Court of Justice. The protection of such rights, whilst inspired by the constitutional traditions common to the Member States, must be ensured within the framework of the structure and objectives of the Community.

Hoechst AG v Commission Cases 46/87 and 227/88

The Commission, exercising its powers under the Competition Regulation (EEC) 917/62 arrived unannounced at H's business premises to obtain information. (The Commission suspected H of operating in a cartel in breach of Article 81 EC (ex 85).) H refused access to his premises without a warrant, which the Commission officials duly obtained. However, the Commission issued a further Decision imposing a financial penalty on H for refusing to comply with its original Decision.

Held The Court held that the Commission must respect fundamental rights when it investigates under the EC competition rules. Article 14 of Regulation (EEC) 17/62 cannot be interpreted in such a way as to give rise to results which are incompatible with the general principles of Community law and in particular fundamental rights. However, on the facts there was no breach of the principles invoked.

National Panasonic (UK) Ltd v Commission Case 136/79

The Commission Decision authorising an investigation into the business affairs of National Panasonic was challenged under Article 230 EC (ex 173). NP had received no informal request for information from the Commission or any advance notice of the Commission's intention to take the Decision. The first NP knew of the Decision was when a Commission official conducted an investigation on NP's premises (the so called 'dawn raid') without waiting for NP's solicitors to arrive. NP claimed that the Commission Decision breached their fundamental right to privacy.

Held The ECJ held that the Regulations which gave the Commission power to carry out such investigations and take Decisions did not refer to respect for any fundamental rights.

9.4   Proportionality

Fédération Charbonnière de Belgique v High Authority Case 8/55
Held The High Authority, when dealing with a breach of the ECSC Treaty, must do so in a manner in proportion to the breach. This is the first time that the Court refers to the notion of the means being in proportion to the ends.

> Note ────────────────────────────────────
>
> The principle of proportionality requires that the means employed to achieve a particular aim are appropriate in relation to the importance of that aim and that they are necessary for the achievement of that aim. The principle of proportionality is now expressly referred to in the Treaty in Article 5 EC (ex 3b) which states that: 'Any action by the Community shall not go beyond what is necessary to achieve the objectives of this Treaty.'

R v Intervention Board for Agricultural Produce ex p Man (Sugar) Ltd Case 181/84
M, a British sugar trader, paid a deposit of £1,670,370 to the Intervention Board as part of the application for an export license. The application was lodged with the board four hours later than the deadline. According to the relevant Community Regulation (EEC) 1880/83, the full deposit was to be forfeited. M claimed that this penalty was disproportionate in relation to the small default on his part.

Held The ECJ, on a reference from the English court concerning the validity of the EEC Regulation, held that the forfeiture of the entire deposit was disproportionate for a minor breach of the deadline. The obligation to apply for an export licence could be enforced by other less drastic means.

Officier van Justitie v De Peijper (Centrafarm BV) Case 104/75
Dutch regulations required that an importer of pharmaceutical goods could not supply a pharmaceutical preparation without the consent of the Chief Public Health Inspector and had to produce documents relating to the composition and manufacture of the products (some of these were documents from the manufacturer). Criminal charges were brought against Centrafarm on the basis that they had imported products from the UK without consent and had failed to have the proper documents. In defence, the company argued that the Dutch regulations were contrary to Article 28 EC (ex 30) (free movement of goods – see Chapter 12).

Held The measures may only be justifiable under Article 30 EC (ex 36) if it is clear that the rules are *necessary* for the effective protection of health and life of humans.

Walter Rau Lebensmittelwerke v De Smedt PvbA Case 261/81

Belgian law required margarine to be packed in cube shaped boxes. The purported aim was that consumers would be able to be distinguish between butter and margarine. The action was brought by a German seller of margarine. A ruling was sought asking whether the Belgian rule was compatible with Article 28 EC (ex 30).

Held The rule was a measure having equivalent effect to a quantitative restriction, contrary to Article 28 EC (ex 30). It could not be justified since the purported aim could have been achieved by other means, such as labelling. (For further discussion, see Chapter 12.)

Pastoors v Belgium Case C-29/95

This case involved Belgian legislation implementing Community rules on the use of tachographs in commercial vehicles. Under Belgian law, offenders could choose between an on the spot fine or criminal proceedings. If an offender elected criminal proceedings, but was not a resident of Belgium, he was required to deposit a sum of money which was greater than the standard fine or face the prospect of having his vehicle impounded. The Belgian authorities asserted this was necessary because it was difficult to enforce criminal proceedings against non-residents.

Held The ECJ held, on a preliminary ruling, that the Belgian rules breached Article 12 EC (ex 6) of the Treaty (which prohibits discrimination based upon nationality). The ECJ also rejected the arguments put forward by the Belgian authorities on the basis that the rules were disproportionate and contrary to the principle of equality.

9.5   Equality

Royal Scholten-Honig (Holdings) Ltd v Intervention Board for Agricultural Produce (Isoglucose Cases) Cases 103 and 145/77

RSHH Ltd were glucose producers. They (along with other glucose producers) challenged a system which provided subsidies for sugar producers. The subsidies were partly financed from a levy imposed on glucose producers. RSHH argued that the system of subsidies was discriminatory since sugar and glucose were competing products, and that the EC Regulations which set up the system were invalid as they breached the principle of equality.

Held The ECJ, in the context of a preliminary ruling from the English court, held that the Regulation was invalid.

Airola v Commission Case 21/74

Held The Court held that Community was bound by the principle of equal treatment of men and women in the treatment of personnel working for the Community.

Pastoors v Belgium Case C-29/95

For facts, see above, 9.4.

Held The Belgian rules breached the fundamental principle of equality.

P v S and Cornwall County Council Case C-13/94

P was dismissed from his council job by his boss, S. He was dismissed because he intended to have a sex change operation. P argued before the industrial tribunal that this was a breach of Directive 76/207/EEC, which deals with equal treatment for men and women in relation to employment.

Held On a preliminary ruling, the ECJ held that the Directive was an expression of the principle of equality which was one of the fundamental principles of Community law, and that the right not to be discriminated against on the grounds of sex was a fundamental human right. The Court stated that the principle should be given a wide interpretation and applied equally to persons who were undergoing a sex change.

Note ───

In *Grant v South West Trains Ltd* Case C-249/96, the ECJ held that the principle of equality did not (at that time) extend to discrimination based on sexual orientation. However, the Treaty of Amsterdam makes specific provision for this form of discrimination. For further discussion, see Chapter 15.

───

The equality principle does not apply in situations which are not similar

Les Assurances du Crédit SA v Council Case C-63/89

Held The ECJ held that the equality principle will not apply in situations which are objectively different.

9.6   Legal certainty

9.6.1   Principle of non-retroactivity

IRCA v Amministrazione delle Finanze dello Stato Case 7/76

The Commission took a Decision to retroactively decrease the level of financial compensation payable on the import of certain products. This was challenged by an Italian importer in proceedings before the Italian courts which sought a preliminary ruling on the validity of the Commission Decision.

Held Where a provision of the Treaty directly authorises the Council or the Commission to legislate, the institutions, like national Parliaments, are free to legislate retroactively. However, the presumption is that they will not. '[A]cts will be held to have retroactive effect only if and in so far as their terms evince, either expressly or by necessary implication, a clear intention that they should have that effect.' Further, the Commission cannot legislate retroactively without the authorisation of the Council.

Société pour l'Exportation des Sucres v Commission Case 88/76

On 30 June 1976, the Commission passed a Regulation which withdrew the right of exporters to cancel their export licences. Although the date of the Regulation was stated as 1 July, the Regulation did not appear in the Official Journal until 2 July, due to industrial action. The applicant applied for cancellation of their export licence on 1 July, but they were refused on the basis of the Regulation.

Held The ECJ held that the Regulation did not come into force until the date it appeared in the Official Journal, 2 July, and did not take effect retrospectively.

R v Kent Kirk Case 63/83

K, the captain of a Danish fishing boat, was charged and fined with fishing in British waters, contrary to a 1982 order. A subsequent EC Council Regulation retroactively authorised the provisions of the UK law. K argued that the retroactive effect of the Council Regulation was not justified because it did not respect the legitimate expectations of those concerned.

Held On a referral from the Crown Court, the ECJ held that the principle of non-retroactivity of penal liability, as enshrined in Article 7 of the ECHR, could not be violated. The Court stated that a national measure in the sphere of Community law, which breaches this right, would be invalid.

Officier van Justitie v Kolpinghuis Nijmegen Case 80/86

KN was prosecuted for selling mineral water which contained additives contrary to Directive 80/777/EEC. However, the Dutch Government had not implemented the Directive. Since a Member State cannot plead the provisions of an unimplemented Directive as against an individual, the national court was forced to take into account the provisions of national law. One of the questions referred to the ECJ was how far the national court must take account of a Directive as an aid to interpretation.

Held The obligation placed upon national courts, to interpret implementing legislation in the light of the Directive (see *Von Colson* – Chapter 8), was limited by the principle of non-retroactivity.

The ECJ can limit the effect of its own judgments in 'exceptional cases'

Defrenne v SABENA (No 2) Case 43/75

D worked for SABENA Airlines as stewardess. She received less pay than the male stewards who were doing the same work. D brought a claim for equal pay in the Belgian courts and sought to rely on the provisions of Article 141 EC (ex 119) of the Treaty.

Held In the light of the exceptional circumstances, the Court would limit its ruling on the direct effect of Article 141 (ex 119). This Article was only directly effective from that point onwards (that is, it could not be directly effective retrospectively to support other claims of equal pay, unless a worker had already commenced legal proceedings). In this case, the Court was limiting the effect of its own judgment because of considerations of legal certainty, but stated that this was an exceptional case.

Barra v Belgium Case 309/85

Held The ECJ held that the normal approach of the Court is to declare the law as it has always been (in other words, retrospectively) and that the approach adopted in *Defrenne* was exceptional. The *Defrenne* approach was reserved for exceptional cases where the Court introduces a new principle, or when the judgment might cause serious difficulties in relation to past events.

Barber v Guardian Royal Exchange Case C-262/88

B, who was made redundant at the age of 52, was refused an early retirement pension under his employer's pension scheme because such a pension was only available to men made redundant after the age of 55. The rules were different for women who were entitled to an early retirement pension at the age of 50. B argued that this was contrary to Article 141 EC (ex 119).

Held The pension scheme was 'pay' and, therefore, covered by Article 141 EC (ex 119). The discrimination between men and women was discriminatory and in breach of Article 141 EC (ex 119). Although the Court held Article 141 EC (ex 119) was directly effective, it also clearly stated that its decision in this case was prospective only.

9.6.2 Legitimate expectation

An expectation will only be legitimate if it is reasonable

Einführ und Vorratsstelle für Getreide und Futtermittel v Mackprang Case 2/75

A Commission decision prevented M, a German grain dealer, from taking advantage of a fall in the value of the French franc and buying cheap grain in France and selling it on profitably to the German Intervention Board, EVGF. M brought an action against EVGF arguing that he had a legitimate expectation of being able to sell the grain to the board.

Held The ECJ, on a preliminary ruling from the German court, held that the Commission's decision did not amount to an infringement of legitimate expectations since it was a justified prevention against speculative activities.

Mulder v Minister van Landbouw en Visserj Case 120/86

M, a Dutch farmer, had received compensation payments from the Commission for five years in return for not producing milk, under the auspices of a Council Regulation designed to prevent the overproduction of milk. A later Council Regulation allocating milk quotas to farmers failed to take into account farmers like M who had participated in the compensation scheme. Consequently, M did not obtain a milk quota and went out of business.

Held The ECJ held that the latter Council Regulation was invalid in that it had failed to take into account the legitimate expectation of farmers such as M. They were entitled to expect to be able to resume production upon the expiry of their original undertaking.

9.7   Procedural rights

9.7.1   The right to a hearing

Transocean Marine Paint Association v Commission Case 17/74

TMPA sought annulment of a Commission Decision which was addressed to them but which did not refer to a condition that was later applied by the Commission in a competition case.

Annulled The ECJ annulled part of the Commission Decision which it held to be in breach of the principle that a person, whose interests are perceptibly affected by a public decision, has the right to be heard and make their own views known.

Hoffman-La Roche & Co AG v Commission Case 85/76

This case was largely concerned with HLR's anti-competitive behaviour which was under investigation by the Commission. In the context of the case, the Commission's procedures were brought into question, in particular concerning the rights of the party under investigation.

Held The ECJ held that the right to be heard is a fundamental right in instances where the public authority can impose penalties.

9.7.2   The duty to give reasons

Union Nationale des Entraîneurs et Cadres Techniques Professionels de Football (UNECTEF) v Heylens Case 222/86

H, a Belgian, was charged in France with practising as a football trainer without the requisite French diploma or equivalent. He had applied to the French authorities for recognition of his Belgian diploma in football training, but they had refused to recognise it and had failed to give any reasons.

Held A decision not to recognise qualification as equivalent, which prevents the free movement of persons under Article 39 EC (ex 48), should be accompanied by the reasons for the decision.

9.7.3 The right to due process

Johnston v Chief Constable of the Royal Ulster Constabulary Case 222/84
Johnston sought to rely on Directive 76/207/EEC to challenge the RUC Chief Constable's rules that men should carry firearms but that women should not, and that women should not be assigned to general police duties. J's contract was not renewed in line with this policy. J claimed that the rule was contrary to Directive 76/207/EEC. She was issued a certificate by the Secretary of State for Northern Ireland stating the decision was conclusive.

Held Directive 76/207/EEC requires Member States to allow for claims to be pursued by judicial process after recourse to the competent authorities. The ECJ held that a compliance certificate of the sort given to J deprived an individual of access to the courts and that an individual has a right to effective judicial protection when asserting rights under Community law.

9.8   Importance of general principles

General principles may be used as an aid to interpretation

Commission v Germany Case 249/86
This case concerned the way in which Germany had implemented provisions relating to Regulation (EEC) 1612/68. Under this Regulation, the families of migrant workers are entitled to entry into another Member State with the worker provided that the worker has accommodation 'considered as normal' for workers of the host Member State. In Germany, the accommodation requirement extended beyond the time of entry to include the entire period of residence.

Held In an Article 226 EC (ex 169) action against Germany, the ECJ held that Regulation (EEC) 1612/68 must be interpreted in the light of the requirement of respect for family life set out in Article 8 of the ECHR. Provided that the worker's family is living in suitable housing when the worker starts work in the host Member State, there is no need for this condition to continue.

Note ───
See also *AM & S Europe Ltd v Commission*, below.

General principles may be used as grounds to challenge EC action under various Treaty Articles (Articles 226, 230, 234 and 241 EC (ex 169, 173, 177 and 184))

Nold KG v Commission Case 4/73

N, a German coal wholesale company, challenged a Commission Decision under the ECSC Treaty on the grounds that the Decision violated the company's right to the free pursuit of economic activity.

AM & S Europe Ltd v Commission Case 155/79

AM & S brought an action for judicial review under Article 230 (ex 173), challenging a Commission Decision which required the company to produce documents which would help the Commission carry out an investigation under the Competition Regulation (EEC) 17/62. In particular, they claimed that the confidential correspondence between themselves and their lawyers should not be disclosed on the grounds of legal professional privilege, a principle common to all Member States.

Held Community rules must take into account the principles and concepts common to the laws of the Member States concerning legal professional privilege. Although the scope of the protection varies between the States, there are common criteria. Regulation (EEC) 17/62 must be interpreted as protecting the confidentiality of written communications between lawyer and client.

United Kingdom v Council Case C-84/94

This was a an Article 230 (ex 173) action brought by the UK concerning the Working Time Directive 93/104/EEC. The UK opposed the Directive and argued that the Directive was wrongly enacted under Article 138 EC (ex 118a) (which deals with health and safety at work and requires a qualified majority vote in the Council). Wishing to preserve its veto in the Council, the UK argued that the Directive should have been adopted under other Treaty Articles (90 and 308 EC (ex 100 and 235)) which require unanimity in the Council. The UK also asserted that the Directive was contrary to the principle of proportionality, in that its provision went beyond that which was necessary.

Held The ECJ held that the Directive had been validly enacted under Article 138 EC (ex 118a). The Court then addressed the issue of proportionality and said:

> As regards the principle of proportionality, the Court has held that, in order to establish whether a provision of Community law complies with that principle, it must be ascertained whether the means which it employs are suitable for the purpose of achieving the desired objective and whether they go beyond what is necessary to achieve it.

On the facts, the Court held that the institutions had not breached the principle of proportionality.

To challenge the action of Member States where the action arises out of an obligation under Community law

Hubert Wachauf v Bundesampt für Ehrnahrung und Forstwirtschaft Case 5/88

A German order implementing the provisions of a Community Regulation concerned with milk production quotas denied compensation to tenant farmers, such as W, where they sought to surrender the quota without the consent of their landlord. In W's case, consent was withdrawn and he was not entitled to any compensation. The Regulation stated that compensation should be paid if the quota was surrendered to the State.

Held Where a Community measure incorporates the protection of a fundamental right, national implementing rules must also give effect in such a way as to respect that right. The German court held that the German order was void because it went against the principle of equal treatment. W was subsequently awarded compensation.

10 Creation of a Customs Union and Discriminatory Internal Taxation

10.1 Creation of a Customs Union and the prohibition between Member States of customs duties on imports and exports or charges having equivalent effect (Article 25 EC (ex 12))

10.1.1 Article 25 EC (ex 12) are directly effective

Algemene Transport-en Expeditie Onderneming Van Gend en Loos NV v Nederlandse Administratie der Belastingen Case 26/62

For facts, see above, 7.1.

Held Article 25 EC (ex 12), which prohibits Member States from introducing, between themselves, duties or charges having equivalent effect, is directly effective and can be enforced by an individual in the national courts.

10.1.2 The ECJ is concerned with the effect on trade of the duty or charge, not the purpose

Commission v Italy (Re Export of Art Treasures) Case 7/68

The Commission brought Article 226 EC (ex 169) proceedings against Italy in respect of a tax imposed on the export of certain artistic and historical items, arguing that the tax was a charge having equivalent effect to a customs duty and, therefore, was in breach of Article 16 (now repealed). In response, the Italian Government argued that the items were not goods (see Chapter 11 for further discussion) and that the tax was not covered by Article 16 (now repealed) since the purpose of the tax was to protect the historical and artistic heritage of the country, and not to raise revenue.

Held The ECJ held that the Treaty does not make any distinction based on the purpose of the duties and charges. The disputed tax fell within Article 16 (now repealed) because export trade is hindered by the pecuniary burden imposed on the price of the exported articles. Any charge which alters the price of exported articles has the same restrictive effect as a customs duty.

10.1.3 Article 25 EC (ex 12) may apply even if the customs duties are not directly imposed by the State

E Dubois et Fils SA and General Cargo Services v Garoner Explotation SA Case C-16/94

GE owned an international road station near Paris, where the customs authorities held offices. ED and GCS, forwarding agents, refused to pay a 'transit charge' imposed on them by GE for each of their vehicles completing customs clearance at the station, arguing it was in breach of Articles 23 and 25 EC (ex 9 and 12). The purpose of the charge was to offset GE's costs in having the customs authorities on their premises.

Held Articles 23 and 25 EC (ex 9 and 12) applied to transit charges. This was so even though it was designed to compensate a private undertaking for bearing costs arising from the customs authorities fulfilling their duties as providers of services in the public interest. The charge was not imposed by the State, but arose from an agreement concluded by the private undertaking (GE) with its customers (ED and GCS).

10.1.4 A charge need not be levied at a border to have an equivalent effect to a customs duty

Steinike und Weinlig v Bundesamt für Ernährung und Forstwirtschaft Case 78/86

Held The ECJ held that a charge need not be levied at a border. Providing that a charge is levied because goods cross a border, it will still be a charge having equivalent effect to a customs duty.

10.1.5 A customs duty levied at a regional frontier may still infringe Article 25 EC (ex 12)

Lancry and Others v Direction Générale des Douanes and Others Cases C-363, 407–11/93

This case concerned 'dock dues' imposed on all goods, whatever their country of origin, imported into the French overseas departments, such as Martinique. The dues were even imposed on goods originating in mainland France itself. The objective was to raise revenue and encourage the local economy. Lancry, which marketed flour in Martinique, imported *inter alia* from France challenged the dues.

Held The ECJ held that Article 23 (ex 9) was infringed. It did not depend on inter-State trade. A charge levied at a regional frontier undermined the unity of the customs union and constituted an obstacle to the free movement 'at least as serious' as charges levied at national frontiers. There were assumed not to be any internal obstacles within Member States, therefore, Article 23 (ex 9) *et seq* makes express reference only to inter-State trade.

10.2 Meaning of 'charges having equivalent effect to a customs duty'

10.2.1 Any charge which is imposed on goods by reason of the fact that they cross a frontier

Commission v Italy (Re Statistical Levy) Case 24/68
Italy imposed a very small levy on goods imported and exported to and from Italy. The purpose of the levy was to fund the collection of trade statistics, which the Italian Government argued would benefit traders.

Held ECJ held that customs duties or charges having equivalent effect were prohibited, regardless of the reason for imposing them:

... any pecuniary charge, however small and whatever its designation and mode of application, which is imposed unilaterally on domestic or foreign goods by reason of the fact that they cross a frontier, and which is not a customs duty in the strict sense, constitutes a charge having equivalent effect within the meanings of Articles 9, 12, 13 and 16 of the Treaty, even if it is not imposed for the benefit of the State, is not discriminatory or protective in effect and if the product on which the charge is imposed is not in competition with any domestic product.

The charge was held to be in breach of Article 12.

Note —————
Articles 9 and 12 are renumbered as Articles 23 and 25 EC. Articles 13 and 16 are now repealed.

Sociaal Fonds voor de Diamantarbeiders v Brachfield Cases 2 and 3/69
Under Belgian law, a charge of less than 0.5% of the value of imported diamonds was paid into a social fund to support workers in the diamond industry. Since Belgium did not produce diamonds, the charge was clearly not protectionist.

Held Despite its purpose, the charge was held to be a charge having equivalent effect to a customs duty because it was imposed on goods by virtue of the fact that they were imported.

Note —————
The ECJ is making it clear that it is concerned with the *effect* on trade of the charge, not the purpose.

10.2.2 No need for the measure to be protectionist

See *Sociaal Fonds voor de Diamantarbeiders v Brachfield* Cases 2 and 3/69, above.

The levy was clearly not a protectionist measure, but was still held to be a charge having equivalent effect to a customs duty.

Commission v Italy (Re Statistical Levy) Case 24/68

Italy levied a small (10 lire) charge on imports and exports. The purpose of the levy was to fund statistical surveys relating to patterns of trade. The ECJ held that since there was no obvious benefit to the individual traders, the levy was a charge equivalent to a customs duty. Any charge, no matter how small, levied by reason of the fact that goods cross a border, and which is not a customs duty in the strict sense, constitutes a charge having equivalent effect, even if it is not imposed for the benefit of the State, is not discriminatory or protective in effect and even if the product on which the charge is imposed is not in competition with any domestic product.

Commission v Luxembourg and Belgium Cases 2 and 3/62

The Luxembourg and Belgian Governments introduced a special import duty on imported gingerbread. They claimed that the purpose of the special duty was to equate the price of foreign gingerbread with domestic gingerbread, which was more highly priced due to a high internal rate of taxation on rye, an ingredient of gingerbread.

Held Whatever it is called, and whatever its mode of application, a charge may be regarded as having equivalent effect to a customs duty if it meets all of the following three conditions:

(1) it must be imposed unilaterally either at the time of import or subsequently;

(2) it must be imposed specifically upon a product imported from a Member State to the exclusion of a similar domestic product; and

(3) by altering the price of the imported product, the charge has the same effect on the free movement of goods as a customs duty.

The special import duty was a charge having equivalent effect to a customs duty.

10.3 Charges for services rendered

10.3.1 There must be an obvious benefit to the trader

Commission v Belgium (Re Customs Warehouses) Case 132/82

The Belgian authorities imposed storage charges upon goods stored at public warehouses prior to the completion of customs formalities. The charge was also imposed on imported goods which were presented at the warehouses solely for customs clearance (that is, where the importer had not requested that the goods be stored). The question was whether such charges had equivalent effect to a customs duty, or whether they were charges for services rendered, as the Belgian authorities argued.

Held The ECJ that, although the use of public warehouses offered certain advantages to importers, such advantages are linked solely with the completion of customs formalities which are always compulsory. Consequently, when payment of storage charges is demanded solely in connection with the completion of customs formalities at a special store, it cannot be regarded as payment for a service actually rendered to the importer. Belgium was held to be in breach of Articles 23 and 25 (ex 9 and 12).

10.3.2 The sum charged for a service rendered must be proportionate to the benefit

Commission v Denmark Case 158/82

Held The ECJ held that, where a genuine service is provided which benefits the importer, a charge may be made, but it must be proportionate to the benefit of the service provided.

Ford España v Spain Case 170/88

Held A sum charged must be proportionate to the cost of providing the service. In this case, the ECJ held that a charge based on the value of goods was not permitted since it was not proportionate to the cost.

10.4 Charges imposed in respect of health inspections

Rewe-Zentralfinanz GmbH v Direktor der Landwirtschaftskammer Westfalen-Lippe Case 39/73

The German authorities imposed a charge on importers in respect of phyto-sanitary inspections of imported apples.

Held The charges were held to be contrary to the Treaty (in this particular case, Article 13 (now repealed)). The health inspections were imposed in the general interest of the public and could not be regarded as a service rendered to the importer. Consequently, the authorities could not impose a charge in respect of these inspections.

Bresciani v Amministrazione Italiana delle Finanze Case 87/75

Charges were levied in respect of compulsory veterinary and public health inspections of imported raw cowhides.

Held The ECJ held that the inspections, imposed in the general interest, could not be regarded as a service rendered to the importer and, as such, the inspection fee constituted a charge having equivalent effect to a customs duty.

10.4.1 Charges rendered in respect of mandatory inspections

Bauhuis v Netherlands Case 46/76

Held In this case, the ECJ held that, where an inspection is mandatory under Community law, a Member State may make a charge to cover the costs of the inspection.

Commission v Germany Case 18/87

German authorities charged fees to cover inspections on live animals which were necessary to comply with the requirements of Directive 81/389/EEC.

Held The ECJ held that these charges were not charges having equivalent effect to a customs duty because they satisfied the following requirements:

(a) charges or fees did not exceed the cost of the actual inspections;

(b) the inspections were mandatory and uniform for all products;

(c) the inspections were provided for by Community law (that is, under the Directive); and

(d) the inspections promoted the free movement of goods.

10.4.2 Inspections permitted under Community law

Commission v Belgium (Re Health Inspection Services) Case 314/82

The Belgian authorities imposed a fee on importers to cover the costs of inspections on imported poultry meat. The Belgian authorities argued that the charge was not a charge having equivalent effect to a customs duty because the health inspections were permitted by Directive 71/118/EEC.

Held The ECJ held that, where an inspection is *permitted* by Community law, as opposed to being mandatory, any fees charged by the Member State would contravene Article 25 EC (ex 12).

10.5 Charges applied to both imported and domestic goods must be applied in the same way

Marimex Spa v Italian Minister of Finance Case 29/72

A tax in respect of a veterinary inspection was applied to both domestic and imported meat. The purpose was to ensure compliance with Italian health standards. However, the inspections and corresponding tax on imported meat were effected by different organisations using different criteria to that for domestic meat.

Held This was in breach of Article 23 EC (ex 9).

10.6 Charges imposed exclusively on domestically produced goods

Apple and Pear Development Council v KJ Lewis Case 222/82

The Apple and Pear Development Council had been set up to promote the consumption of apples and pears grown in England and Wales. Lewis refused to pay the levy due to fund the APDC and was sued by the Council. In Lewis's defence, it was argued that the activities of the APDC were contrary to Community law.

Held Since the levy did not apply to imported products, there was no breach of Articles 23 or 25 EC (ex 9 and 12). However, a levy may be unlawful if it breaches other Treaty provisions, namely, Article 28 EC (ex 30). (For further discussion of this case, see Chapter 11.)

10.7 A charge applied exclusively for the benefit of domestic goods

Capolongo v Azienda Agricola Maya Case 77/72

A charge was imposed by the Italian Government on egg boxes, whether they were domestically produced or imported. The purpose of the charge was to support the manufacture of paper and cardboard in Italy.

Held The ECJ held that the charge was in breach of Article 13 (now repealed). Although the charge applied without discrimination, it was held to be discriminatory since the purpose of the charge was to support domestic products.

10.8 Article 90 (ex 95) – prohibition on discriminatory internal taxation

10.8.1 What is a genuine tax?

Commission v France (Re Levy on Reprographic Machines) Case 90/79

The Commission brought this action against France arguing that, in imposing a levy on reprographic machines, France had breached Article 90 EC (ex 95). The tax was imposed on all reprographic machines irrespective of origin but, in fact, no such machines were made in France.

Held The ECJ defined a tax as a:

> ... genuine system of internal dues applied systematically to categories of products in accordance with objective criteria irrespective of origin of the products.

A genuine tax may be imposed on imported goods even where the importing state does not produce identical or similar products.

Co-operativa Co-Frutta Srl v Amministrazione delle Finanze dello Stato Case 193/85

An importer of bananas into Italy challenged an Italian tax imposed on bananas. The tax was imposed on imported and domestically grown bananas, but, since Italy does not grow a significant quantity of bananas, the tax fell largely on imported bananas. There was no similar tax on other types of fruit. The Italian court had to consider whether the tax was a charge having equivalent effect to a customs duty (under Article 25 EC (ex 12)) or a tax under Article 90 EC (ex 95).

The ECJ contrasted a charge having equivalent effect to a customs duty with an internal tax. The essential feature of the first is that it is borne solely by an imported product, whilst the latter is borne both by domestic and imported goods.

Held The tax in issue was held to be an integral part of a general system of internal dues within the meaning of Article 95.

Steinike und Weinlig v Bundesamt für Ernährung und Forstwirtschaft Case 78/86

Held The ECJ held that:

> ... financial charges within a general system of internal taxation applying systematically to domestic and imported products according to the same criteria are not to be considered charges having equivalent effect.

Denkavit v France Case 132/78

A charge was imposed on a consignment of lard imported from Germany into France.

Held The ECJ held that, in order for a charge to be part of a system of internal taxation, the charge on the imported product must be the same as the charge on a domestic product. The charge must be taxed at the same rate and it must be imposed at the same stage in the marketing chain.

10.8.2 Prohibition of direct discrimination

Lütticke (Alfons) GMBH v Hauptzollamt Saarlouis Case 57/65 [1966] ECR 205

The German authorities imposed a special tax (a turnover equalisation tax) from Lütticke in respect of a consignment of powdered milk imported by Lütticke into Germany from Luxembourg. Domestically produced powdered milk was not subject to this tax.

Held The ECJ held that this constituted a directly discriminatory tax and was in breach of Article 90 EC (ex 95). In this case, the ECJ held that Article 90 EC (ex 95) was capable of direct effect.

Note

Member States rarely impose taxes which are directly discriminatory. It is more frequent for a Member State to impose taxes which are indirectly discriminatory.

10.8.3 Prohibition of indirect discrimination

Humblot v Directeur des Services Fiscaux Case 112/84

H challenged the system of annual car tax in France when he imported his 36 CV car. The annual tax on cars in France was split into two different levels. For cars below 16 CV, the tax level increased progressively up to a maximum of 1,100 francs. For cars above 16 CV, there was a flat rate of 5,000 francs. Since all French manufactured cars were below 16 CV, they were subject to the lower tax rate, whereas more powerful imported cars were subject to the much higher tax rate. The basis of H's claim was that the different tax bands were discriminatory and contrary to Article 90 EC (ex 95).

Held The ECJ held that, although the tax system did not place a formal distinction between imported and domestic cars, it was manifestly discriminatory, because the high power rating could only affect imported cars, whereas domestic cars were subject to a distinctly more advantageous tax rate. The system was protectionist.

Mölkerei-Zentrale v Hauptzollamt Paderborn Case 28/67

In the context of a preliminary ruling from a German court, the ECJ was asked to interpret the phrase 'internal taxation imposed indirectly on similar products'.

Held The ECJ held that the words directly or indirectly must be given a wide interpretation to include taxes imposed on domestic products at various stages of the manufacturing and marketing process.

Commission v Ireland (Re Excise Payments) Case 55/79

In this case, the Irish Government imposed the same rates of tax on imported and domestically produced alcoholic drinks. However, the tax on imported drinks was levied at the time the goods were imported, whereas domestic producers benefited from a deferment of payment and did not need to pay the tax until some four to six weeks later, when the goods were put on the market.

Held that, although the benefit to national producers was small, the application of this system was obviously discriminatory. The ECJ stated that, in assessing whether a tax is discriminatory, it is necessary to consider the actual effect of the tax on national production, compared to the effect on imported goods. Even where the tax rate is the same, the detailed rules for assessment and levying must be taken into account.

10.8.4 What is a 'similar' product?

Commission v France (Re French Taxation of Spirits) Case 168/78

This case involved French legislation which imposed a higher rate of taxation on grain based spirits (such as whiskey and gin, which were

91

largely imported) than on fruit based spirits (such as cognac and calvados, which were largely home produced). The French authorities argued that these products were not similar, whereas the Commission asserted that they were.

Held The ECJ held that it is necessary to interpret the concept of 'similar products' with flexibility and that it must be interpreted widely. In deciding whether products are similar, it is necessary to consider whether they have similar characteristics and meet the same needs from the point of view of the consumer. In this case, it was held that the spirits were similar and that the French provisions contravened Article 90 EC (ex 95).

John Walker and Sons Ltd v Ministeriet for Skatter og Afgifter Case 243/83
In this case, John Walker (a Scotch Whiskey producer) challenged the Danish legislation which imposed a higher rate of tax on whiskey than on fruit wines of the liqueur type.

Held In order for goods to be consider as 'similar', it is necessary to compare certain objective characteristics of both categories of beverage, such as their origin, method of manufacture, taste and alcohol content, and also to consider whether or not both categories of beverages are capable of meeting the same needs from the point of view of the consumer. It was held that whiskey was not similar to fruit liqueur wines because the alcoholic strength of whiskey was twice as great as that of the fruit liqueurs.

10.9 Article 90(2) EC (ex 95(2)) – taxation affording indirect protection to domestic products

Commission v UK (Re Tax on Beer and Wine) Case 170/78
In the UK, the internal tax rate for wine was £3.25 per gallon, whereas beer was taxed at only £0.61 per gallon. The Commission brought an action against the UK arguing that the UK tax on wines was protective of the UK beer market. In the UK, most wine is imported, unlike beer, which is largely domestically produced. The Commission argued that the different rates of taxation were contrary to Article 90(2) EC (ex 95(2)), in that they afforded indirect protection for domestic goods.

Note ———————————————————————————————————————

The Commission had to rely on Art 90(2) EC (ex 95(2)) since the goods in question were not similar.

Held Article 90(2) EEC (ex 95(2)) applies to goods which, whilst not similar, are partially or potentially in competition with imported goods. In considering whether a competitive relationship exists, it is necessary to consider both the present state of the market and also possible future developments and the potential for substitution of products. After considering detailed information supplied by the Commission, the Court held that beer was in competition with certain wines at the cheaper end of the market (still light wines made from fresh grapes) and, consequently, that the UK had breached Article 90(2) EC (ex 95(2)).

Different tax rates may be applied providing the difference is based upon objective criteria

Commission v France Case 196/85

Under the French tax system, different rates of tax applied to natural sweet wines (whose production was traditional and customary) and other kinds of liqueurs and wines. The French authorities argued that the tax advantage gained by these traditionally produced wines was offset by the severe conditions under which these wines were produced (low rainfall and poor soil) and that the tax was necessary to sustain output in certain regions.

Held The ECJ held that the differential treatment was justified as it was part of an economic policy to provide support to certain regions.

11 The Free Movement of Goods: Articles 28 and 29 EC (ex 30 and 34) – the Prohibition of Quantitative Restrictions on Imports and Exports and All Measures having Equivalent Effect

11.1 The meaning of 'goods'

11.1.1 Goods are products which can be valued in money and can form the subject of commercial transactions

Commission v Italy (Re Export Tax on Art Treasures) Case 7/68
Article 226 EC (ex 169) case brought by the Commission against the Italian State. The Commission considered that a tax on the export of certain articles of artistic and historic interest was in breach of Article 16 (now repealed) of the Treaty. The Italian State argued that the tax applied to specific artistic works which could not be described as 'goods' and therefore could not be subject to the provisions of the Treaty.

Held The ECJ held that 'products which can be valued in money and which are capable, as such, of the forming the subject of commercial transactions' are goods within the meaning of the Treaty. The artistic works were held to be goods.

11.1.2 Money is not goods

R v Thompson, Johnson and Woodiwiss Case 7/78
In this case the ECJ was asked to consider whether coins could constitute goods or whether they were capital.

Held The Court held that if the coins are legal tender then they are not goods and therefore not subject to the Treaty provisions relating to the freedom of movement of goods.

Bordessa and Others Cases C-358 and 416/93

B was stopped at Gerona on the Spanish-French border driving through the 'nothing to declare' channel. He had 50 million pesetas hidden in his car. According to Spanish law, authorisation was required for the export of notes in excess of 5 million pesetas per person per journey.

Held The ECJ held that the exportation of bank notes was not governed by Article 28 EC (ex 30) (or indeed Article 49 EC (ex 59) – see Chapter 14), but fell to be considered under Article 67 (now repealed) concerning the free movement of capital.

11.1.3 Goods supplied in a contract for works are goods within Article 28 EC (ex 30)

Commission v Ireland (Dundalk Water Supply) Case 45/87

In a contract for the construction of a water supply scheme, Dundalk District Council included a requirement that the pressure pipes complied with an Irish standard specification. A company was advised that there was no point in bidding for the contract if they intended to use pipes manufactured in Spain. In proceedings brought by the Commission the Irish Government argued that the contract was not for the supply of goods but a works contract and therefore not subject to Article 28 EC (ex 30).

Held The ECJ held that Article 28 EC (ex 30) also applies to goods supplied under a contract for services.

11.1.4 Waste is goods

Commission v Belgium Case C-2/90

A Belgian decree prohibited the discharge or dumping of waste coming from other States. The Commission brought Article 226 EC (ex 169) proceedings against Belgium arguing, *inter alia*, that the Belgian provisions were contrary to Article 28 EC (ex 30).

Held Waste, whether it could be recycled or not, was to be regarded as goods within the meaning of the Treaty and therefore subject to the free movement provisions.

> [O]bjects which are transported over a frontier in order to give rise to commercial transactions are subject to Article 30 [now 28 EC], irrespective of the nature of these transactions.

11.2 Prohibition of quantitative restrictions

Riseria Luigi Geddo v Ente Nazionale Risi Case 2/73

The ECJ defined a quantitative restriction as a ' total or partial restraint of import, exports or goods in transit'.

R v Henn and Darby Case 34/79

A UK law banning hardcore pornography was held by the ECJ on a reference from the House of Lords to be an extreme example of a quantitative restriction.

Commission v Italy (Re Ban on Pigmeat) Case 7/61

A ban on the import of pork into Italy was held to be a quantitative restriction.

Salgoil SpA v Italian Minister of Foreign Trade Case 13/68

Held The ECJ held that a system of import quotas was also a breach of Article 28 EC (ex 30) in that it was a quantitative restriction on imports.

11.3   Measures having equivalent effect to quantitative restrictions: the *Dassonville* formula

Procureur du Roi v Dassonville Case 8/74

Dassonville was a trader in Belgium who imported a consignment of scotch whisky from France. Under Belgian law, spirits were required to be accompanied by a certificate of origin. Since the consignment had been imported from France, where the whisky was in free circulation, it was difficult for D to obtain this certificate of origin. He forged labels on the bottles and was charged with a criminal offence in the Belgian courts. In his defence, he argued that the certificate of origin requirement amounted to a measure having equivalent effect to a quantitative restriction and, accordingly, contravened Article 28 EC (ex 30).

Held The ECJ held that the certificate of origin requirement was a measure having equivalent effect to a quantitative measure. This Belgian requirement clearly hindered trade in that traders importing products that had been put into free circulation in another Member State would find it more difficult to obtain the certificate of origin than those traders importing directly from the country of origin. The ECJ provided the classic definition of 'measures having equivalent effect to a quantitative measure' as:

> ... all trading rules enacted by a Member State which are capable of hindering, directly or indirectly, actually or potentially, intra-Community trade.

This has become known as the '*Dassonville* formula'.

> Note ─────────────────────────────
> This is a good example of an individual seeking to rely on the direct effect of a Treaty provision against the State.

11.4 Examples of measures having equivalent effect to quantitative restrictions

11.4.1 Origin marking

See *Dassonville*, above, 11.3.

Commission v UK (Re Origin Marking) Case 207/83

Certain goods (that is, textiles, electrical goods) were required by UK law to be marked with, or accompanied by, an indication of origin. The rule was indistinctly applicable in that it applied to all goods, domestic and imported alike.

Held The law infringed Article 28 EC (ex 30). The purpose of origin marking is to enable consumers to distinguish between imported and domestic goods and this enables them to assert any prejudices they may have against foreign goods. The UK provisions were also liable to increase the production costs of imported goods, making it more difficult to sell them in the UK market.

Commission v Ireland (Irish Souvenirs) Case 113/80

Legislation in Ireland required that imported souvenirs of Ireland be stamped either with a place of origin or the word 'foreign'. No equivalent requirement was placed on souvenirs made in Ireland.

Held The ECJ held that the Irish legislation infringed Article 28 EC (ex 30), in that it was a measure having equivalent effect to a quantitative restriction.

11.4.2 'Buy national' campaigns

Commission v Ireland (Re Buy Irish Campaign) Case 249/81

In 1978 the Irish Government started a promotional campaign specifically to encourage the promotion of Irish goods. The Irish Goods Council, sponsored by the government, was given responsibility for promoting Irish goods on the basis of their Irish origin.

Held The ECJ held in Article 226 EC (ex 169) proceedings that the campaign promoting Irish goods was in breach of Article 28 EC (ex 30), its intention being to substitute domestic products for imported products in the Irish market and thereby check the flow of imports from other Member States.

This case was distinguished in *Apple and Pear Development Council v Lewis*.

Apple and Pear Development Council v Lewis Case 222/82

The Apple and Pear Development Council had been set up to promote the consumption of apples and pears grown in England and Wales. In order to do this, they advertised using slogans such as 'Polish up your English'. L refused to pay the levy due to fund the APDC and was sued by the Council. In L's defence, it was argued that the activities of the APDC breached Article 28 EC (ex 30).

Held There was no breach of Article 28 EC (ex 30). It is permissible to promote a national product by reference to its particular qualities but not simply because it is from a particular State.

Meat and Livestock Commission v Manchester Wholesale Meat and Poultry Market Ltd (1997)

The case concerned the 'recipe for love' advertising campaign in the UK. In particular, each advert bore the logo 'British Meat'.

Moses J, in the Queen's Bench Division, held that references to British meat in the campaign as a whole were insignificant in comparison to references to the qualities of that meat (for example, versatility, ease of preparation, healthiness) and were not sufficient to be capable of arousing 'chauvinistic or xenophobic emotions in the consumer'.

Held The campaign was not in breach of Article 28 EC (ex 30).

11.4.3   Restricting the use of certain names to domestic goods

Ministère Public v Deserbais Case 286/86

Under French law 'Edam' cheese was required to have a minimum fat content of 40%. D imported Edam cheese from Germany which had a fat content of less than 35%. When D marketed the cheese in France as 'Edam' cheese he was prosecuted on the grounds of the unlawful use of the trade name 'Edam'. D argued that the French rule amounted to a breach of Article 28 EC (ex 30).

Held Article 234 EC (ex 177) reference to ECJ. The ECJ held that Article 28 EC (ex 30) prevents Member States from applying national laws, which makes the right to use the trade name subject to compliance with a minimum fat content, to products of the same type lawfully manufactured and sold in another Member State.

Criminal proceedings against Karl Prantl Case 16/83

Under German regulations governing wine, the use of the 'Bocksbeutel' bottle (a bottle with a distinctive shape) was limited to wines from two German regions which had used that particular bottle for centuries. Wine producers from a region in Italy used a similar shaped bottle and had also done so for over a century. Karl Prantl, an Italian, imported the Italian wine into Germany and was charged with a breach of the German regulations.

Held On a reference from the German criminal court, the ECJ held that an exclusive right to use a certain type of bottle, granted by national legislation, cannot be used as a bar to imports of wines in similar bottles. The wines from the originating Member State had been using the same, or similar, bottles according to fair and traditional practice in that Member State.

11.4.4 Marketing rules

Walter Rau Lebensmittelwerke v de Smedt PvbA Case 261/81

Belgian law required margarine to be sold only in a cube shaped form or package. The law was introduced in order to help busy shoppers easily distinguish margarine from butter.

Held Packaging requirements such as these are capable of making it more difficult or more expensive for imported goods to be sold. Such rules may bar certain channels of distribution or may necessitate additional costs in complying with the packaging requirement. As such, the rules were held to be in breach of Article 28 EC (ex 30).

11.4.5 Type approvals

Commission v France Case 21/84

A British manufacturer of postal franking machines complained to the Commission after he had repeatedly failed to obtain the approval of the French authorities for his franking machines. The Commission argued that France had contravened Article 28 EC (ex 30) by refusing to approve machines manufactured in another Member State.

Held An approval system itself could conform with Article 28 EC (ex 30). However, the conduct of the French authorities was in breach of Article 28 EC (ex 30) because it refused, without proper justification, to approve machines from another Member State.

11.4.6 Health inspections

Commission v UK (Re UHT Milk) Case 124/81

A UK requirement stipulated that UHT Milk could only be marketed by approved dairies. The UK Government argued that this was a necessary requirement to ensure that the milk was free from infection. This meant that imported milk had to be repackaged and retreated.

Held ECJ held that this amounted to a measure having an equivalent effect to a quantitative restriction.

Rewe-Zentralfinanz GmbH v Landwirtschaftskammer Case 4/75

Certain plant products, such as apples, imported into Germany were exposed to sanitary inspections. The purpose of the inspections was to prevent the spread of a pest known as San José scale. Domestically grown apples were not subject to comparable compulsory examination.

Held The ECJ held that such inspections which could cause delays and additional transport costs to the importer are likely to make importation more difficult. Accordingly, the Court held that inspections at frontiers may constitute measures having equivalent effect to quantitative restrictions, unless they are justified under Article 30 (ex 36). See Chapter 12 for further discussion.

11.4.7 Requirement to have a licence

Commission v UK (Re Imports of Poultry Meat) Case 40/82

The UK introduced a licensing system for poultry imported from all Member States with the exception of Denmark and Ireland. The licensing system amounted, in practice, to a ban on the import of poultry. The UK argued that the purpose of the system was to prevent the spread of Newcastle Disease, a highly contagious disease which affects poultry.

Held A licensing system may constitute a measure having equivalent effect to a quantitative restriction.

International Fruit Co NV v Produktschap voor Groenten en Fruit (No 2) Cases 51–54/71

Held The ECJ held that even a licensing system which was simply a formality would be a breach of Article 28 EC (ex 30).

11.4.8 Price maintenance

Openbaar Ministerie v Van Tiggele Case 82/77

Criminal proceedings were brought against VT for selling gin at a price below the national fixed minimum price.

Held The ECJ held that a fixed minimum price, even where it applies to domestic and imported goods alike, is capable of hindering cheaper imported goods, which are unable to be sold at their lower price.

Criminal proceedings against Tasca Case 65/75

T was charged with selling sugar at a price higher than that permitted under Italian law, which specified a maximum price.

Held The ECJ held that an indistinctly applicable fixed maximum price only becomes a measure having equivalent effect to a quantitative restriction where the price level makes it more difficult, or impossible, for imported goods to be sold.

11.5 Article 28 EC (ex 30) is not subject to a *de minimis* rule

Criminal proceedings against Jan de Haar Cases 177 and 178/82

A Dutch court sought a reference from the ECJ asking whether Dutch excise law relating to the resale of tobacco products could be regarded as a measure having equivalent effect to a quantitative restriction. It only restricted imports to a very small degree and imported goods could be marketed in other ways.

Held The ECJ made it clear that even if a hindrance to trade is slight, and even if it is possible for imported goods to be marketed in other ways, a rule or measure could still be in breach of Article 28 EC (ex 30) if it is capable of hindering imports. The Court was effectively saying that Article 28 EC (ex 30) is not subject to any *de minimis* rule.

11.6   Selling arrangements

Cases prior to Keck

Oebel Case 155/80
Belgian law, aimed at protecting workers in small and medium-sized bakeries, prohibited the production and delivery of baking products during night time hours.

   Held The ECJ held that this rule did not contravene Article 28 EC (ex 30) since it did not hinder trade within the Community which remained possible at all times.

Blesgen v Belgium Case 75/81
Belgian law prohibited the consumption of strong spirits in public bars.

   Held Although most spirits sold in Belgium are imported, the ECJ held there was no breach of Article 28 EC (ex 30). Trade would not be affected because people could still buy spirits to drink at home.

Quietlynn Ltd v Southend Borough Council Case C-23/89
Under UK law, the sale of certain sex appliances (including some imported goods) in sex shops was prohibited unless licensed.

   Held The ECJ held that the licensing requirement did not infringe Article 28 EC (ex 30) since the goods in question could be sold through other outlets and channels, such as mail order, or in shops where such items constitute a minor part of the stock in trade.

11.7   The Sunday trading cases

National rules regulating the freedom of retailers to trade on Sundays have caused particular problems. These rules were discussed in the following 'Sunday trading cases'.

Torfaen Borough Council v B & Q plc Case 145/88
This was one of the first cases concerned with the Sunday trading rules in England and Wales. B & Q were charged by the council for Sunday trading in contravention of the provisions of the Shops Act 1950. In their defence, B & Q argued that the legislation and the ban on Sunday trading amounted to a measure having equivalent effect to a quantitative restriction. (Another good example of an individual seeking to rely on the provisions of the Treaty in their defence in a criminal prosecution.)

Held The ECJ held that the law was *prima facie* in breach of Article 28 EC (ex 30), but accepted that such laws were justifiable. Article 28 EC (ex 30) did not apply to national Sunday trading rules where the restrictive effects on Community trade which may result do not exceed the effects intrinsic to rules of that kind. The ECJ left it to the national courts to decide whether the rules were proportionate to their aims.

Note

The result of this led to considerable confusion. It was unclear what the exact purpose of the Shops Act 1950 was.

B & Q Ltd v Shrewsbury and Atcham Borough Council (1990)

Here, the magistrate's court held that the purpose of the Act was to protect workers from being forced to work on Sundays and, accordingly, the Act was disproportionate and infringed Article 28 EC (ex 30).

Torfaen Borough Council v B & Q plc Case 145/88

Here, the national court thought the purpose of the Act was to 'preserve the traditional character of the British Sunday' and that the Act achieved this and did not do more than was necessary.

Stoke on Trent City Council v B & Q plc Case C-169/91

Held The ECJ held that the Shops Act 1950 was proportional and lawful. The Sunday trading legislation was justified on the basis of 'national or regional socio-cultural characteristics' under the rule of reason (which will be discussed in Chapter 12). The law was also proportionate.

Note

The law has now been clarified by the following case.

11.8 *Keck* – a move away from the wide application of the *Dassonville* formula

Keck and Mithouard Cases C-267 and 268/91

French legislation prohibited the resale of goods that had not been altered in any way, at a price below the original purchase price (effectively prohibiting resale at a loss). K and M were both charged with breaching this law and, in their defence to the charges, they argued that the French law was contrary to Article 28 EC (ex 30).

Held The ECJ stated that the French legislation could potentially restrict the volume of sales of goods from other Member States and, as such, following *Dassonville*, was a measure having equivalent effect to a quantitative restriction. However, the court held that, 'contrary to what has previously been decided', it would not be, provided that the 'provisions apply to all affected traders operating within the national territory and provided that they affect in the same manner, in law and in fact, the marketing of domestic products and of those from other Member States'.

In other words, selling arrangements will not breach Article 28 EC (ex 30) if they do not hinder trade in imports any more than they hinder trade in domestic goods. A measure must have some discriminatory effect, for example putting the imported goods at a disadvantage re domestically produced goods.

Tankstation't Heukste vof and Boermans Cases C-401 and 402/92

A preliminary ruling was sought in a Dutch case concerning the compatibility with Article 28 EC (ex 30) of Dutch rules governing the times and places at which petrol could be sold.

Held The ECJ held that Article 28 EC (ex 30) did not apply to rules concerning the compulsory closing of petrol retail outlets. The Dutch rules applied to all petrol retailers throughout the Netherlands. Whilst affecting the volume of sales, the rules did not discriminate between domestic and imported goods.

The new direction in Keck *applies to advertising as well as selling arrangements*

Hunermund v Landesapothekerkammer Baden-Württemburg Case C-292/92

German rules, laid down by the professional body, banned pharmacists from advertising on the radio, on TV or at the cinema. They were allowed to advertise in newspapers and magazines, but could only state the name, address and phone number of the practice plus the name of the proprietor. The aim was to prevent excessive competition between pharmacists. H, a pharmacist, objected, arguing a breach of Article 28 EC (ex 30).

Held Applying the new direction laid down in *Keck*, the ECJ held there was no breach of Article 28 EC (ex 30). The German rules applied to all pharmaceutical products; there was no discrimination at all. Thus, the rule in *Keck* concerning selling arrangements was extended to advertising.

Leclerc v TFI and M6 Case C-412/93

French law prohibited advertising on TV of certain products and services, such as alcohol over 1.2% proof and the distribution sector. The aim was to force these sectors to advertise in regional newspapers instead, thereby protecting regional newspapers. L, petrol distributors, were denied access to French TV advertising by TFI and M6, advertising companies. L argued that the French law was incompatible with Article 28 EC (ex 30).

Held The ECJ held that Article 28 EC (ex 30) did not apply to the French law.

Groupement National des Négociants en Pommes de Terres de Belgique (Belgapom) v ITM Belgium SA and Vocarex SA Case C-63/94

Belgian law on Commercial Practices and Consumer Protection 1991 prohibited traders from offering a product for sale, or selling a product at a loss. This occurred in any sale where 'the price is not at least equal to the price at which the product was invoiced at the time of supply...'. The law further provided that 'Any sale, which taking account of those prices and overheads, yields only a very low profit margin is to be treated as a sale at a loss'.

V, a franchisee of ITM, bought a consignment of potatoes at 27 Belgian francs per 25 kg and resold them at 29 Belgian francs per 25 kg, making a gross profit of only 1.3% of the purchase price. B objected, since all other Belgian outlets had agreed to sell at 89 francs. V argued, in his defence, that the rule was contrary to Article 28 EC (ex 30) in that it constituted a measure having equivalent effect to a quantitative restriction.

Held The ECJ held that Article 28 EC (ex 30) did not apply to this situation, applying *Keck, Hunermund* and *Leclerc*.

11.9 Article 28 EC (ex 30) is addressed to Member States and relates to measures taken by Member States

The State however has been given a very wide meaning. It includes:

- national and local government, in its many forms;
- semi-public bodies such as quangos (see *Apple and Pear Development Council v KJ Lewis*, above, 11.4.2);
- the Post Office (see *Commission v France (Re Franking Machines)* Case 21/84);
- the police force (see *R v Chief Constable of Sussex ex p International Trader's Ferry Ltd*, below);
- regulatory agencies and professional bodies (see *R v Royal Pharmaceutical Society of Great Britain* Cases 266 and 267/87).

Commission v Ireland (Re Buy Irish Campaign) Case 249/81

The activities of the Irish Goods Council, a Government sponsored semi-public body given the task of promoting Irish goods on the basis of their Irish origin, infringed Article 28 EC (ex 30). Although the Council could not adopt legally binding measures, it could influence Irish traders and shoppers into discriminating against Irish goods. The campaign was developed ultimately at the initiative of the Irish Government.

R v Chief Constable of Sussex ex p International Trader's Ferry Ltd (1995)

Animal rights protesters were campaigning against live animal exports across the Channel through the port of Shoreham, Sussex. Despite the campaign, exports were able to continue. In April 1995, however, the Chief Constable, concerned that the financial and manpower resources being committed to policing the port were interfering with the effective policing of the county generally, decided to reduce the level of policing. This meant that on certain days of the week no police were present at the port, and they turned back livestock vehicles if it was thought a breach of the peace might otherwise occur.

ITF sought to have the decision of the Chief Constable quashed. The High Court held that since the decision only applied to livestock due for export from the UK to other Member States, it was a *prima facie* breach of Article 29 EC (ex 34). Furthermore, the police could not rely on the effect of civil disturbance as affording a public policy defence under Article 30 EC (ex 36), where resources were available to deal with such disturbances and the cost of doing so was not disproportionate.

11.9.1 Member States are under a positive obligation to ensure the free movement of goods

Commission v France (Re French Farmers) Case C-265/95

In this case, the French farmers had been attacking, damaging and threatening foreign lorries and their drivers. Their aim was to stop imported agricultural products getting into France.

Held The ECJ held that the French Government, in 'manifestly and persistently' failing to take adequate and appropriate measures to stop the French farmers, had contributed to an obstacle to the free movement of goods. The Court stated that Article 28 EC (ex 30) applies 'where a Member State abstains from adopting the measures required in order to deal with obstacles to the free movement of goods which are not caused by the State'. Hence, it was held that the French Government had breached Article 28 EC (ex 30) and Article 10 EC (ex 5).

11.9.2 Article 28 EC (ex 30) also applies to action taken by the Community institutions

Meyhui v Schott Zwiesel Glaswerke Case C-51/93

Directive 69/493/EEC, on the approximation of laws relating to crystal glass, required that descriptions on crystal glass products had to appear only in the language(s) of the country in which they were to be sold. This was challenged under Article 28 EC (ex 30).

Held Article 28 EC (ex 30) was infringed as it would require manufacturers to use different labelling for different countries, thus increasing costs. However, it was justified under *Cassis*, as being necessary for consumer protection. Consumers could not readily distinguish different quality glass and, therefore, the clearest information possible was required so that consumers would not mistakenly pay too much for inferior quality glass.

11.10 Article 29 EC (ex 34)

Groenveld BV v Produktschap voor Vee en Vlees Case 15/79
Under Dutch law, manufacturers of meat products were prohibited from stocking or using horse meat. The purpose of the ban was to enable the export of processed meats to countries, such as the UK, where the sale of horse meat is prohibited. G argued that this rule infringed Article 29 EC (ex 34).

Held The ECJ held that there had been no breach of Article 29 EC (ex 34), even though other less restrictive methods, such as labelling, could have been used, because the object of the law was not to restrict exports.

Germany v Deutsches Milch-Kontor Case C-426/92
German law required skimmed milk powder, due for export before being processed into animal feed, to be subject to systematic inspections at the German frontiers. This was challenged on the grounds that it was breach of Article 29 EC (ex 34).

Held The ECJ held that the inspections amounted to a measure having equivalent effect to a quantitative restriction on exports.

Procureur de la Republique v Bouhelier Case 53/76
Held French rules which required quality inspections on watches destined for export, but not on those for the French market, were held to be in breach of Article 29 EC (ex 34).

12 The Free Movement of Goods – the Rule of Reason and Article 30 EC (ex 36)

Note ———————————————————————————————————————
One of the most confusing consequences of the Treaty renumbering is that Article 36 is now Article 30. Students of EC law need to take considerable care to ensure that they know which Treaty Article they are referring to.

12.1 *Cassis de Dijon* – the rule of reason

Rewe-Zentrale AG v Bundesmonopolverwaltung für Branntwein Case 120/78

German legislation laid down a minimum alcohol level of 25% per litre for certain spirits including Cassis de Dijon. German cassis conformed to this level but French *cassis* did not, having an alcohol level of 15–20%. Although the German measure applied to all spirits, domestically produced or imported (*indistinctly applicable*), it had the effect of prohibiting the sale of French cassis. The German measure was challenged by some German importers.

Held On a reference from the German court, the ECJ held that the measure had equivalent effect to a quantitative restriction. However, the Court went on to say that *in the absence of Community rules relating to the production and marketing* of products, certain measures may be acceptable if the measures are *necessary* to satisfy *mandatory requirements*:

> Obstacles to movement within the Community resulting from disparities between the national laws relating to the marketing of the products in question must be accepted in so far as these provisions may be recognised as being necessary in order to satisfy mandatory requirements relating in particular to the effectiveness of fiscal supervision, the protection of public health, the fairness of commercial transaction and the defence of the consumer.

This is known as the 'rule of reason'.

The ECJ also established the second *Cassis de Dijon* principle, sometimes known as the principle of mutual recognition.

12.1.1 *Cassis de Dijon* – the mutual recognition principle

Following on from its judgment above, the ECJ went on to state that provided goods have been lawfully produced and marketed in one Member State there should be no valid reason why they should not be introduced into any other Member State. This is known as the mutual recognition principle.

This means there is a presumption in favour of the free movement of goods. A Member State may rebut this presumption if it can show that the national measures are necessary to meet one of the mandatory requirements.

Note ───

See, also, *Ministère Public v Deserbais* Case 286/86, below, 12.2.1, as an example of the ECJ applying the mutual recognition principle.

12.2 The mandatory requirements

12.2.1 The protection of public health

Rewe-Zentrale AG v Bundesmonopolverwaltung für Branntwein (Cassis de Dijon) Case 120/78

For facts, see above, 12.1. The German authorities argued that the measures were introduced to protect public health. (An interesting argument based on the idea that low alcohol drinks lead to a greater tolerance for alcohol and cause alcoholism.)

Held The ECJ rejected this claim. The ban was unnecessary (disproportionate) and, in any event, the German public could already purchase a very wide range of weakly or moderately alcoholic products.

Ministère Public v Deserbais Case 286/86

Under French law cheese could be sold as 'Edam' unless it had a minimum fat content of 40%. D imported Edam cheese from Germany which was lawfully produced and sold in Germany but had a fat content of less than 35%. D was prosecuted in France for the unlawful use of the trade name Edam. In his defence D argued that the French rule was unlawful under Article 28 EC (ex 30). There were no Community rules concerning this subject.

Held ECJ held that a Member State cannot restrict the use of a trade name, such as Edam, to goods with a minimum fat content where cheese products of a similar type have been lawfully made and marketed under that name in another Member State. The Court went on to say that the French rules could not be justified under the rule of reason, since consumers could be informed about the fat content of the cheese by appropriate labelling.

Note ───

This case demonstrates both the mutual recognition principle and the principle of proportionality.

───

Commission v Germany (Re German Beer Purity) Case 178/84

Under German law, the use of additives in beer was prohibited and Germany did not allow the marketing of any beer in Germany which did not comply with the German standards. The use of such additives was authorised in other Member States. The Commission brought Article 226 EC (ex 169) proceedings and the German Government argued that the ban was necessary to stop the use of the additives in beer, which was consumed in 'considerable quantities' by the German public. The German authorities sought to justify the rules as being necessary to protect public health.

Held The ECJ found that the German rules were in breach of Article 28 EC (ex 30) and could not be justified in the interests of public health. The Court had regard to the findings of the international scientific community, the World Health Organisation and the EEC's own Scientific Committee for Foods. It also stated that the German rules were disproportionate (see below).

12.2.2 The defence of the consumer

Commission v Germany (Re German Beer Purity) Case 178/84

The German beer rules also stated that the use of the name 'Bier' could only be used where the drink was brewed from only malted barley, hops, yeast and water. The German Government argued that this rule was necessary to protect German consumers, because they linked the word 'Bier' with drinks manufactured solely from the above ingredients.

Held The German designation of 'Bier' could not be restricted to beers manufactured in accordance with the German rules. The Court recognised that it is legitimate to seek to protect consumers where they link specific qualities to beers made from particular ingredients. However, the Court emphasised that such objectives should be ensured in a way which does not prevent the import of products lawfully manufactured and sold in other Member States. The ECJ held that the German rules were disproportionate and that the consumer could be suitably informed (and therefore protected) by adequate labelling. The German State was held to be in breach of Article 28 EC (ex 30).

Meyhui v Schott Zwiesel Glaswerke Case C-51/93

Directive 69/493/EEC, on the approximation of laws relating to crystal glass, included a requirement that the descriptions on crystal glass products had to appear only in the language(s) of the country in which they were to be sold.

Held Article 28 EC (ex 30) was infringed, as it would require manufacturers to use different labelling for different countries, increasing costs of production. However, it was justified under *Cassis*, as being necessary for consumer protection. Consumers could not readily distinguish different qualities of glass, and therefore the clearest information possible was required, so that consumers would not mistakenly pay too much for inferior quality glass.

Verein gegen Unwesen in Handel v Mars Case C-470/93

Mars produced a variety of ice cream bars, including Mars Bars, Snickers, Bounty and Milky Way, in France, and imported them into Germany. All the bars were marked '+ 10%'. The German Trade Association claimed that this was in breach of German law on unfair competition, which prohibits the giving of misleading information about products on two grounds:

(1) consumers would think the price was unchanged (that is, that it was '10% extra free'; and

(2) the band bearing the '+ 10%' sign was much wider than the volume of the bar which represented the actual extra 10%.

In their defence, Mars claimed the German law was in breach of Article 28 EC (ex 30).

Held The ECJ held that the law was in breach of Article 28 EC (ex 30) and that the mutual recognition principle (see above at 12.1.1) applied, as the ice creams were lawfully manufactured and marketed in France. The Court rejected arguments that the rules were justified as being necessary in the interests of consumer protection. This was on the grounds that the price of the bars had not in fact been increased and the width of the band bearing the '+ 10%' sign would not mislead the reasonably circumspect consumer.

Note ───

In *Cassis de Dijon*, the German Government sought to justify its measures under a number of these heads. How did the ECJ respond to these arguments?

12.3 Extension of the mandatory requirements since *Cassis*

12.3.1 The improvement of working conditions

Oebel Case 155/80

This case concerned a Belgian law banning the production and delivery of bread to consumers and retailers during the night hours, designed to protect workers in Belgian bakeries from being forced to work nightshifts.

Held The rule did not breach Article 28 EC (ex 30) because trade within the Community remained possible at all times. However, the Court appeared to recognise that the improvement of working conditions could constitute a mandatory requirement.

Union Départmentale des Syndicats CGT de l'Aisne v SIDEF Conforama Case C-312/89
Held The ECJ held that legislation for the protection of workers could constitute a mandatory requirement.

12.3.2 Cultural activities

Cinéthèque SA v Fédération Nationale des Cinémas Français Cases 60 and 61/84
French legislation, designed to protect the French film industry, prohibited the marketing of videos of films during the first year of the film's release. The rule applied to all films whether they were made in France or not (indistinctly applicable).

Held The ECJ held that it was possible for measures designed to protect cultural activities to be justified under the rule of reason.

12.3.3 The protection of the environment

Commission v Denmark (Re Danish Bottles) Case 302/86
The Danish Government, concerned about the environmental consequences of litter and waste from discarded metal cans, instituted a system requiring beer and soft drinks to be marketed only in containers that could be re-used. The use of metal cans was forbidden. Containers needed to meet the requirements laid down and be approved by the Danish National Agency for the Protection of the Environment. Non-approved containers were permitted subject to very strict limits and to a deposit and return system. Although the object of the system was to reduce the numbers of discarded metal cans, it had as an effect a potential restriction on competition. Manufacturers of beers and soft drinks outside Denmark could sell their products throughout the Community but not in Denmark unless they could comply with the deposit and return system.

Held The ECJ held that the approval system was incompatible with Article 28 EC (ex 30) but accepted that the deposit-and-return system was lawful. In reaching its conclusions, the Court clearly stated that 'the protection of the environment is a mandatory requirement which may limit the application of Article 30 [now 28 EC] of the Treaty'. The approval system was contrary to the principle of proportionality.

12.3.4 National and regional socio-cultural characteristics

Torfaen Borough Council v B & Q plc Case 145/88

This was one of the so called 'Sunday trading cases' (see Chapter 11). Section 47 of the Shops Act 1950 prohibited Sunday trading in the UK. When charged with a breach of this Act, B & Q argued that the Act was a breach of Article 28 (ex 30).

Held the ECJ held that the law was *prima facie* in breach of Article 28 EC (ex 30), but accepted that such rules were justifiable, because the purpose of such rules was to ensure that working and non-working hours are arranged in accordance with national or regional socio-cultural characteristics. In the absence of Community rules, this is a matter to be determined by the Member States. The ECJ however referred the matter back to the domestic court to determine whether the rules were necessary (proportional).

(The subject of selling arrangements was considered in more detail in Chapter 11.)

12.3.5 The prevention of fraud

Germany v Deutsches Milch-Kontor Case C-426/92

German law required skimmed milk powder, due for export before being processed into animal feed, to be subject to systematic inspections at the German frontiers. This was challenged under Article 29 EC (ex 34).

Held The inspections amounted to a measure having equivalent effect to a quantitative restriction on exports. However, random spot checks were permissible in the interests of the prevention of fraud. This would appear to be a new mandatory requirement.

12.3.6 Maintenance of press diversity

Vereinigte Familiapress Zeitungsverlags und Vertriebs GmbH v Heinrich Bauer Verlag Case C-368/95

HBV, a German publisher, published a weekly magazine which it sold in Germany and Austria. The magazine contained various puzzles with cash prizes. Austrian legislation prohibited magazine publishers from including prize competitions in their magazines. VFZ, an Austrian newspaper publisher, brought an action in the Austrian courts seeking an order to prevent HBV from distributing in Austria. According to the Austrian Government, the rule was necessary to protect small publishers whose survival could be threatened by big publishers running competitions with big prizes.

Held The ECJ held that, if there was a competitive relationship between such publishers the rule would not breach Article 28 EC (ex 30). The ECJ established that maintenance of press diversity was a mandatory requirement. However, such rules must still be proportional.

12.4 Measures justified under the rule of reason must be proportional

Walter Rau Lebensmittelwerke v De Smedt PvbA Case 261/81

According to Belgian law, margarine was required to be packed into cube shaped boxes. The Belgian Government argued that this trading rule was necessary in the interests of the consumer as it enabled them to distinguish between margarine and butter. However, the ECJ held the Belgian rule was in breach of Article 28 EC (ex 30). The interests of the consumer could have been secured by more proportional means, namely labelling.

Although the Court agreed that legislation designed to prevent butter and margarine from being confused in the mind of the consumer is justified, the Court went on to say that the requirement that the packaging of margarine in a cubic package (to the exclusion of other types of packaging) 'exceeds the requirements of the object in view'. The rules were held to be disproportionate because consumers may, in fact, be protected just as effectively by other less restrictive measures, such as labelling.

12.5 The rule of reason applies only to indistinctly applicable measures

Italian State v Gilli and Andres Case 788/79

Under Italian law, vinegar was required to be made from the fermentation of wine. G and A were charged with fraud when they attempted to sell apple vinegar, imported from Germany, in Italy. There was no Community law governing the subject. In their defence, G and A argued that the Italian rule was contrary to Article 28 EC (ex 30).

Held The ECJ held that the rule was contrary to Article 28 EC (ex 30) and could only be justified if it fell under one of the mandatory heads. On the facts, the Court determined that the rules were not necessary to secure the protection of health since apple vinegar was not harmful. However, the Court went on to suggest that the rule of reason exception to Article 28 EC (ex 30) applied only to indistinctly applicable national measures (measures applying without discrimination to both imported and domestic goods).

Note ———————————————————————————————

Hence, a national measure which is distinctly applicable (applies only to imported goods) can only be justified under Article 30 EC (ex 36).

———————————————————————————————

Commission v Ireland (Irish Souvenirs) Case 113/80

Legislation in Ireland required that imported souvenirs of Ireland be stamped either with a place of origin or the word 'foreign'. No equivalent requirement was placed on souvenirs made in Ireland and, therefore, the measure was distinctly applicable. The Commission brought proceedings under Article 226 EC (ex 169). The Irish Government tried to justify the measure under the rule of reason.

Held The ECJ held that, because the measure was distinctly applicable, it could not be justified under the principles established in *Cassis de Dijon*. The Court also confirmed that the list of exceptions in Article 30 EC (ex 36) is exhaustive.

12.6 Article 30 EC (ex 36)

12.6.1 Public morality

R v Henn and Darby Case 34/79

The UK banned the import of pornographic materials. Similar material in the UK was only illegal if it was likely to 'deprave or corrupt', but imports were prohibited if they were ' indecent or obscene'. H and D were charged with illegally importing pornographic materials into the UK from Rotterdam. The defendants, H and D argued that the ban constituted arbitrary discrimination because stricter rules applied to imported goods.

Held The ECJ held that, although the ban was in breach of Article 28 EC (ex 30), it could be justified under Article 30 EC (ex 36). The ban was discriminatory but it was not arbitrary. Since there was no lawful trade in the UK of such pornographic materials, this was not a disguised restriction on imports. The measure fell within Article 30 EC (ex 36) because it was imposed to protect public morality and not to protect national products. It is up to Member States to determine the requirements of public morality in their own territory.

Conegate Ltd v Customs and Excise Commissioners Case 121/85

UK Customs and Excise officials prevented inflatable 'love dolls' and other sex aids which had been imported from Germany from entering into the UK. At the time, the sale of these items was restricted in the UK, but there was no ban on either their manufacture or marketing.

Held The ECJ held that the seizure of the goods in question could not be justified under Article 30 EC (ex 36) because there was no ban and because the UK had not taken any effective steps to stop the sale/distribution of such goods. A Member State may not rely on the grounds of public morality to prohibit imports when its own legislation does not prohibit the manufacture or marketing of the same goods on its own territory.

12.6.2 Public policy

R v Thompson, Johnson and Woodiwiss Case 7/78

English coins were unlawfully imported into the UK despite a ban on their import. The coins, which were no longer legal tender, were held to be goods (see Chapter 11) and, *prima facie*, the breach was contrary to Article 28 EC (ex 30).

Held The ban could be justified on the grounds of public policy because the need to protect the right to mint coinage was one of the fundamental interests of society.

Cullet v Centre Leclerc Case 231/83

The French Government set minimum retail prices for fuel. The ECJ held that this was a measure having equivalent effect to a quantitative restriction. The French Government sought to rely on the public policy exception, arguing that if the minimum prices were not maintained there would be civil disorder, including violence.

On the facts, the ECJ rejected the argument, but accepted that public disorder could constitute a grounds for public policy.

12.6.3 Public security

Campus Oil Ltd v Minister for Industry and Energy Case 72/83

Irish law required importers of petroleum products to buy up to 35% of such products from the Irish National Petroleum Company at fixed prices.

Held Even though the measure was clearly in breach of Article 28 EC (ex 30) and the Treaty competition provisions, it was justified on the grounds of public security. The Court accepted the Irish Government's arguments that such a measure was necessary to maintain the continued viability of the only petroleum refinery in Ireland. This was essential in the event of a national crisis.

Note ──

The Court also accepted that the measure could be justified on the grounds of public policy.

12.6.4 Protection of the health and life of humans, animals and plants

Rewe Zentralfinanz GmbH v Landwirtschaftskammer Case 4/75

In Germany, imported apples were made subject to inspection. The purpose of the inspection was to allow the Member State to control a pest (called San José scale).

Held The ECJ held, in this case, that the inspection was necessary because the imported apples constituted a real risk of the pest which did not exist in domestic apples.

Commission v UK (Re UHT Milk) (Case 124/81)

A UK requirement stipulated that UHT milk could only be marketed by approved dairies. The UK Government argued that this was a necessary requirement to ensure that the milk was free from infection. This meant that imported milk had to be repackaged and retreated.

Held The ECJ held that the UK measure could not be justified under Article 30 EC (ex 36) since it was clear that milk from Member States was of a similar quality and was also subject to equivalent controls.

Commission v France (Re Italian Table Wines) Case 42/82

French customs officers carried out systematic checks on three quarters of each consignment of Italian wine. Checks on French wine transported in France were far less frequent.

Held The French were not justified in carrying such systematic checks and that random checks would suffice unless there was any suspicion based on specific evidence that greater checks should take place in a given case.

Officier van Justitie v Sandoz BV Case 174/82

S was charged by the Dutch authorities with selling muesli bars which contained added vitamins. Under Dutch law, muesli bars could not contain added vitamins because, it was argued, excessive vitamin intake could be unhealthy. Therefore, the Dutch authorities sought to justify their rules under Article 30 EC (ex 36) – the protection of human health. It should be noted that muesli bars with added vitamins were lawfully sold in other Member States and that there was no conclusive scientific evidence about the exact level at which vitamin intake becomes unhealthy.

Held In the absence of conclusive scientific evidence, national rules which prohibit, without prior authorisation, the sale of certain foods which have added vitamins are justified under Article 30 EC (ex 36) providing the rules are proportional.

Ministère Public v Claude Muller and Others Case 304/84

A French law restricted the use of E475, an emulsifying agent in foods and in particular bread. It was argued that this law could restrict the importation of food from Germany, where the agent was widely used in foodstuffs.

Held The French law was justifiable under Article 30 EC (ex 36), taking into account the fact that consumption of bakery products was appreciably higher in France.

R v Home Secretary ex p Evans Medical and Macfarlan Smith Case C-324/93

Diamorphine, a heroin substitute, is used in the UK by hospitals as a painkiller. Prior to 1992, imports of diamorphine into the UK were prohibited, and EM had the only government licence to import concentrated poppy straw powder. MS had the only licence to process that powder into diamorphine. Another firm, Generics, objected that this infringed Article 28 EC (ex 30). The Home Secretary agreed and in 1992 granted G an import licence for diamorphine. EM and MS sought judicial review of this action.

They relied, *inter alia*, on Article 307 (ex 234) (which states that pre-accession agreements between Member States and other non-EU countries are not affected by the Treaty) and that the 1961 Single Convention on Narcotic Drugs, which came into effect in the UK in 1964, took precedence over Article 28 EC (ex 30). The Convention allows the State to limit 'exclusively to medical and scientific purposes the production, manufacture, export, import, distribution of, trade in, use of and possession of drugs' (Article 4(l)).

EM and MS further argued that even if Article 28 EC (ex 30) did apply, the Home Secretary could have relied on Article 30 EC (ex 36).

Held The measures taken by the State to control the import of drugs was subject to Article 28 EC (ex 30), regardless of Article 307 EC (ex 234), because that Article only applied to agreements which were incompatible with the Treaty. The fact that the future viability of EM was at risk was irrelevant as Article 30 EC (ex 36) had no application on economic matters. However, the ECJ accepted that Article 30 EC (ex 36) may be invoked on the ground that import restrictions were necessary to ensure the reliability of supply of diamorphine in the UK. Whether Article 30 EC (ex 36) *was in fact* available depended on whether or not other means, less restrictive of trade, were available.

Ortscheit GmbH v Eurim Pharm Arzneimittel GmbH Case C-320/93

German law prohibited the advertising of medicinal products which had not yet been authorised in Germany. This was challenged in respect of certain products lawfully on sale in other EC States.

Held The German law infringed Article 28 EC (ex 30) (as it deprived doctors and pharmacists of information relating to the availability of new drugs) but was justifiable under Article 30 EC (ex 36), in the interests of public health.

Centre d'Insemination de la Crespelle Case C-232/90

French law requiring imported bovine semen to be delivered to approved insemination centres was upheld under Article 30 EC (ex 36) (protection of health and life of animals).

12.6.5 Protection of national treasures

Commission v Italy (Re Export Tax on Art Treasures) Case 7/68

The ECJ indicated that an intention to prevent the export of art treasures may have been justified under this head. However, this was essentially an *obiter* statement. Article 30 EC (ex 36) will not justify an export tax.

12.6.6 Protection of industrial and commercial property

Centrafarm BV and Adriann de Peijper v Sterling Drug Inc Case 15/74

Sterling Drug, an American company, marketed a medical product called 'Negram'. This was patented by Sterling in the UK and the Netherlands. Centrafarm, a Dutch company, bought Negram in the UK and Germany and then imported it into the Netherlands. Sterling sought to prevent the parallel imports into the Netherlands by invoking their patent rights.

Held The ECJ held that only the specific subject matter of the property can be protected by Article 30 EC (ex 36) when the rights have not already been exhausted by being put into circulation in the EEC.

12.7 Article 30 EC (ex 36) cannot be used to justify commercial interests

Commission v UK (Re Newcastle Disease) Case 40/82

The UK introduced a licensing requirement for imported poultry on the grounds that it was attempting to combat the spread of Newcastle Disease, which affects poultry.

Held The licensing requirement could not be justified. The Court considered that pressure had been brought to bear on the UK Government from domestic poultry breeders who were concerned about increasing imports of poultry from other Member States. In addition, the licensing requirement was timed just before Christmas, when sales of poultry and turkey traditionally increase. The Court decided that the licensing requirement was introduced not to protect public health, but to safeguard commercial interests.

12.8 Measures must not constitute a means of arbitrary discrimination or a disguised restriction on trade between Member States

Commission v Italy (Re Ban on Pork Imports) Case 7/61

Italy prohibited the import of pork and the Commission commenced Article 226 EC (ex 169) proceedings on the grounds that the ban was contrary to Article 28 EC (ex 30). Italy sought to justify the ban on the grounds of public health.

Held The purpose of Article 30 EC (ex 36) is to allow national legislation to derogate from Article 28 EC (ex 30) only to the extent justified in order to achieve one of the objectives set out in Article 30 EC (ex 36). Article 30 EC (ex 36) can not be used to justify a disguised restriction in trade.

Commission v Germany (Re Health Control on Imported Meat) Case 153/78
Held The purpose of Article 30 EC (ex 36) is to permit national legislation to derogate from the free movement of goods only to the extent necessary in order to achieve one of the objectives laid down in Article 30 EC (ex 36).

Note ───

The case of *Conegate Ltd v Customs and Excise*, above, 12.6.1, is a good example of a national measure which is held to be arbitrary discrimination.

12.9 Recourse to Article 30 EC (ex 36) not possible where harmonising Directives necessary to achieve the same objective are in place

R v Ministry of Agriculture, Fisheries and Food ex p Hedley Lomas (Ireland) Ltd Case C-5/94
Between April 1990 and January 1993 the UK's Ministry of Agriculture, Fisheries and Food systematically refused to issue licences for the export to Spain of live animals intended for slaughter. This was because the Ministry was of the view that a number of Spanish slaughterhouses were not complying with Directive 74/557/EEC on the stunning of animals prior to slaughter. Although the Ministry had insufficient evidence as to the overall position in Spanish slaughterhouses, it believed the level of non-compliance with the Directive justified a general ban on export licences.

Hedley Lomas, a firm of animal exporters, was refused a licence to export live sheep to Spain in 1992, even though the firm had information that the particular slaughterhouse for which the sheep were intended was complying with the relevant directives on animal welfare. Hedley Lomas brought an action seeking a declaration that the refusal to issue licences was unlawful, and damages. The Ministry did not deny its refusal was contrary to Article 29 EC (ex 34), but argued that it was justified under Article 30 EC (ex 36).

Held The ECJ held that recourse to Article 30 EC (ex 36) was not possible where harmonising directives necessary to achieve the same objectives were already in place. It was irrelevant that the directives did not lay down Community monitoring procedures, or any penalty for breach, because Member States remained obliged under Article 10 EC (ex 5) of the Treaty to take all measures necessary to guarantee the application of EC law. Member States had to trust each other to carry out inspections in their respective territories. Consequently, the actions of the Ministry constituted a breach of EC law.

13 The Free Movement of Workers: Article 39 EC (ex 48)

13.1 Who is a worker?

Levin v Staatssecretaris van Justitie Case 53/81

L was a British national, living in the Netherlands and married to a national from a non-EC country. She was refused a permit to reside in the Netherlands on the grounds that she had not been in employment for the requisite year before her application. She appealed against that decision in the Dutch courts, arguing that she had sufficient income and that she had taken up part time employment as a chambermaid. The Court sought a preliminary ruling from the ECJ as to whether a person who earned below the subsistence level (as defined by Dutch legislation) could be a 'worker' within the meaning of Article 39 EC (ex 48) of the Treaty.

Held ECJ held that the term 'worker' is a community concept and cannot be defined by reference to national law. The term 'worker' covers those in full time and part time employment and includes those who receive less than a subsistence level. Accordingly, L was a worker. However, the Court stated that, to be a worker, a person must be involved in 'effective and genuine activities'. Activities on such a small scale which are 'purely marginal and ancillary' would not constitute work.

Kempf v Staatssecretaris van Justitie Case 139/85

K was a German national working in the Netherlands. He applied for a residence permit. He was employed as a part time music teacher and received social assistance to supplement his income. K's application was refused on the basis that he was not a worker because he was not able to support himself from his income and had to rely on public funds.

Held The ECJ held that a person in effective and genuine part time employment can not be excluded from the free movement provisions because the pay they receive is below subsistence. It is irrelevant if the supplementary means of subsistence are drawn from public funds.

R v Secchi (1975)

S was an Italian living in London doing odd jobs and shoplifting.

Held He was held not to be a worker because his activities were 'marginal and ancillary'.

Steymann v Staatssecretaris van Justitie Case 196/97

S was a German national working in a Dutch religious community, doing plumbing work and general household duties in return for food and shelter. He was not paid in cash.

Held The ECJ held that if the undertaking to do work was remunerated in tangible benefits, this was sufficient to show that a person was a worker.

Union Royale Belge de Sociétés de Football Association (URBSFA) and Others v Jean-Marc Bosman Case C-415/93

B, a Belgian football player, brought proceedings against the Belgian national professional football association (URBSFA) when he was prevented from taking up a contract with a French football club. Under the transfer rules a nationality clause limited the extent to which foreign players could play for other Member States.

Held The ECJ held that a professional football player was a worker and that the transfer rules were in breach of Article 39 EC (ex 48) (and in breach of the EC competition rules – Articles 81 and 82 EC (ex 85 and 86)).

Bettray v Staatssecretaris van Justitie Case 344/87

B was refused a residence permit from the Dutch authorities on the grounds that he was not a worker. B was staying at a drug rehabilitation centre for drug addicts and was involved in a work scheme for which he received some payment. The aim of the scheme was to assist in drugs rehabilitation.

Held That a person employed under such a scheme, which was principally aimed at rehabilitation or reintegration, is not a worker. The objective of the work could not be regarded as an effective and genuine economic activity.

A trainee is a worker

Lawrie-Blum (Deborah) v Land Baden-Württemberg Case 66/85

In order to become a secondary school teacher in Germany, it was necessary to undertake a period of service training. The national court asked the ECJ whether a trainee teacher undertaking this service training was a worker.

Held The essential feature of an employment relationship is that for a 'certain period of time a person performs services for and under the direction of another person in return for which he receives remuneration'. A trainee teacher did qualify as a worker, applying these criteria.

Bernini v Minister van Onderwijs en Wetenschappen Case C-3/90

This case concerned B, an Italian, who was employed for a period of 10 weeks as a paid trainee.

Held The ECJ held that a worker could work a small number of hours and receive limited wages. However, the ECJ stated that:

> ... a national court can consider, when assessing whether a person provides a genuine and effective service, whether in all the circumstances the person has completed a sufficient number of hours in order to familiarise himself with the work.

A person seeking work is a worker

R v Immigration Appeal Tribunal ex p Antonissen Case C-292/89

A, a Belgian national, entered the UK in October 1984. Six months later, he was sentenced by the Crown Court to two years' imprisonment for possession of drugs. At the time he had still not found employment. The Secretary of State for Home Affairs took a decision to deport A. In judicial review proceedings against the deportation order, the High Court sought a ruling from the ECJ on whether a Member State can deport a person if after six months from entry into the Member State they have failed to find employment.

Held The ECJ held that Article 39 EC (ex 48) should be given a wide interpretation and the freedom of movement of workers also entails the right for nationals of Member States to move within the territory of other Member States and to stay there for the purposes of seeking employment. However, a person may be deported after six months if he has still not found employment.

Hoekstra v BBDA Case 75/63

H, a Dutch worker, became ill during a visit to her family in Germany. She sought to recover the costs of the medical expenses incurred in Germany from a voluntary insurance scheme to which she had made payments. She was refused. In the course of the case which followed in the Dutch courts, a preliminary ruling was sought on the meaning of the term 'wage earner or assimilated worker' in a Council Regulation concerned with social security.

Held The ECJ held that the term 'worker' is a community concept and included a person who, having lost his or her job, is capable of taking another.

13.2 The direct effect of Article 39 EC (ex 48)

Walrave and Koch v Association Union Cycliste Internationale Case 36/74

The rules of the International Cyclist Association required 'pacemakers' in world cycling championships to be of the same nationality as the 'stayers' (those who stayed in the race). The ICA was not a public body or part of the State. The rules were challenged by W and K.

Held The ECJ held that the ICA was bound by Article 39 EC (ex 48). 'Prohibition of such discrimination does not only apply to the action of public authorities but extends likewise to rules of any nature aimed at regulating in a collective manner gainful employment and the provision of services ...' Thus, Article 39 EC (ex 48) is capable of horizontal direct effect.

Union Royale Belge des Sociétés de Football Association and Others v Jean-Marc Bosman Case C-415/93

Under the rules of the Belgian Football Association (URBSFA), a player who refused a new contract was to be placed on a compulsory transfer list, and could only move to a new club without the agreement of his current club subject to the payment of a compensation fee. Jean-Marc Bosman, a Belgian national, was employed as a player with RC Liège, a Belgian first division club, under a contract which expired on 30 June 1990. In April 1990, RC Liège offered him a new contract on a much reduced salary. Bosman refused to sign and was placed on the transfer list. The transfer fee was fixed at 1.7 million Belgian francs.

No club was willing to pay this, and although Bosman secured temporary transfers to various clubs in France, he began court proceedings in April 1992 against RC Liège, URBSFA, and European football's governing body, the Union des Associations Européennes de Football (UEFA), seeking a declaration that the transfer rules were illegal.

He was also seeking a declaration that UEFA's nationality clause was illegal. From the 1960s, many national footballing organisations had introduced rules restricting the number of foreigners who could play in particular games. In 1991, UEFA, following discussion with the Commission, adopted the '3 + 2' rule. According to this rule, national football associations were allowed to limit to three the number of foreign players a club could field in any national championship match, or UEFA-organised cup game, plus two 'affiliated' players, meaning those players who had played in the country for an uninterrupted period of five years.

Held The Belgian court referred the matter to the ECJ, which held firstly that the free movement provisions applied to professional footballers. While pure sporting activities were not governed by Article 39 EC (ex 48), the activities of the players employed by professional clubs gave them the element of economic activity required, following *Walrave and Koch v Association Union Cycliste Internationale* Case 36/74.

Next, the Court held that the transfer rules were an infringement of Article 39 EC (ex 48). However, the Court pointed out that this ruling only applied where a player was out of contract, and wished to transfer to a club in *another Member State*.

The ECJ also held that the nationality clause was an infringement of Article 4(l) of Regulation (EEC) 1612/68. The ECJ rejected various arguments put forward by UEFA, including the fact that the '3 + 2' rule had the approval of the Commission. The Court responded that the Commission had no authority to approve of illegal practices.

13.3 Entry into a Member State to seek employment and Directive 68/360/EEC

R v Immigration Appeal Tribunal ex p Antonissen Case C-292/89

A, a Belgian national, entered the UK in October 1984. He was later sentenced by the Crown Court to two years' imprisonment for possession of drugs. At the time he had still not found employment. The Secretary of State for Home Affairs took a decision to deport A. In judicial review proceedings against the deportation order, the High Court sought a ruling from the ECJ on whether a Member State can deport a person if, after six months from entry into the Member State, they have failed to find employment.

Held The ECJ held that a Member State may be permitted to deport a person who has not found employment within six months, unless the person concerned can provide evidence that he is continuing to seek employment and has genuine chances of being engaged.

Procureur du Roi v Royer Case 48/75

R, a French national living and working in Belgium, was ordered to leave the country by the Belgian police on the grounds that his residence there was unlawful, due to the fact that when he had entered Belgium he had not completed all of the requisite administrative formalities. After leaving Belgium, R returned and was convicted. The Belgian court sought a ruling from the ECJ asking whether failure to comply with administrative formalities could constitute grounds for deportation.

Held A failure to comply with such formalities did not constitute grounds for deportation, but could be enforced by more proportionate penalties. The right to move throughout the Community is based on Article 39 EC (ex 48) and not the residence permit, which is simply to be regarded as proof of the position of a national of another Member State.

Commission v Belgium (Re Treatment of Migrant Workers) Case C-344/95

This case concerned a number of aspects of Belgian law concerned with the treatment of migrant workers:

- nationals of other Member States seeking work in Belgium had to leave the country after three months if they were unsuccessful in getting work. *Held* Following *Antonissen*, it was for a Member State to decide how long non-nationals could stay to look for work, but a person could not be required to leave if they were still seeking work and had a genuine chance of finding some;
- migrant workers were only entitled to a full residence permit after two three month residence certificates had been issued. All of these documents were charged for. *Held* It was a breach of Directive 68/360/EEC not to issue a residence permit immediately. It is possible

to charge for a residence permit. However, on the facts, the charge breached the Directive because it was greater than that imposed on Belgian nationals when applying for a national ID card.

13.3.1 Compliance with reasonable immigration formalities

Watson and Belmann Case 118/75

W, a British national, was touring in Italy. As part of her travels, she was provided with accommodation by B, an Italian national, in return for work as an au pair. Italian law required foreign nationals to report to the police within three days of arrival. W was charged with failing to report to the police and B was charged with failing to inform the authorities within 24 hours of the residence of a foreign national, in accordance with Italian law. Both pleaded that the Italian legislation was inconsistent with Articles 12 EC (ex 6) and 39 EC (ex 48) on the grounds that it constituted discrimination on the grounds of nationality.

Held The ECJ held that Member States were entitled to hold records of foreign nationals entering, residing and leaving the territory. Such requirements did not interfere with the free movement of workers unless they imposed a penalty disproportionate to the offence. Deportation was held to be disproportionate.

Messner Case C-265/88

Held On similar facts, 15 years later, Italian law requiring immigrants to register with the police within three days, enforced by criminal penalties, was held to be disproportionate.

R v Pieck Case 157/79

Stanislaus Pieck, a Dutch worker was prosecuted in England for staying longer than the six month period allowed when his passport had been stamped 'leave to enter for six months'. He did not have a residence permit. P relied on Article 39 EC (ex 48) and argued that the grant of leave to enter was contrary to Community law.

Held The ECJ held that, as long as a worker enjoys the right to enter as a worker, this is not dependent upon a residence permit. The failure of a migrant worker to obtain a residence permit can not be punished by deportation. If a Member State imposes other penalties in respect of non-compliance with formalities, such penalties must be proportionate. The ECJ stated that imprisonment would be disproportionate.

Commission v Belgium Case 321/87

The Commission brought proceedings against Belgium because it argued that the Belgian practice of occasionally asking other EC nationals to show their residence permit when crossing the border was contrary to the free movement provisions.

Held It was not unlawful for a Member State to require immigrants to carry their residence permits for inspection, where an identical obligation is imposed upon its own nationals.

Skanavi and Chryssanthakopoulos Case C-193/94

This case involved criminal proceedings against S and C. S, a Greek national had established a business in Germany. She had not exchanged her Greek driving licence for a German one as she was required to do. She was charged with driving without a licence, which carried a prison sentence or fine.

Held On a preliminary ruling, the ECJ held that the imposition of a criminal penalty was disproportionate. The exchanging of a driving licence is an administrative formality and does not constitute the basis of the right to drive in the host state. The Court considered that the imposition of a criminal penalty would constitute a lasting restriction on the free movement of workers, establishment and services.

13.4 Regulation (EEC) 1612/68 – eligibility for employment and equal treatment

13.4.1 Eligibility for employment

Commission v France Case 167/73

French legislation required a certain percentage of the crew of a ship to be of French nationality.

Held The ECJ held that Article 39 EC (ex 48) was 'directly applicable in the legal system of every Member State'. As such, Article 39 EC (ex 48) will prevail over any contrary domestic legislation. France was held to be in breach of Regulation (EEC) 1612/68.

Groener v Minister for Education Case 379/87

Government policy in Ireland was to promote the use of the Irish language as a means of expressing national identity and culture. A certificate of proficiency in the Irish language was required for certain teaching posts in Ireland. G, a Dutch national, applied for a full time teaching post in Ireland, but did not hold the requisite certificate. She had been teaching in Ireland on a part time basis for two years and had been recommended for the post. However, she was refused it because she failed the test to obtain the certificate. G brought an action against the Minister for Education when he refused to waive the requirements of the certificate.

Held The Treaty does not prohibit Member States from adopting policies designed to protect and promote a language. However, such policies must not infringe the fundamental freedom under Article 39 EC (ex 48) and any measures must be proportionate in relation to the aim of the policy.

13.4.2 Equality of treatment – Article 7(1)

Württembergische Milchverwertung-Südmilch AG v Ugliola Case 15/69

An Italian national was forced to return to Italy from Germany to do national service. His German employer, when calculating the seniority of his staff, only counted periods of national service that had taken place in Germany, although the nationality of the worker was irrelevant. In effect, workers such as U who did their national service outside Germany were treated less favourably.

Held The ECJ held that this was unlawful because it indirectly introduced discrimination in favour of German nationals. U was entitled to the same treatment as a German national would have received.

Sotgiu v Deutsche Bundespost Case 152/73

S, an Italian national living and working in Germany, applied for a separation allowance which was paid by the German Post Office to workers working away from their families. A higher allowance was paid to those employees who had been living in Germany when they had been appointed than was paid to employees who, at the time of recruitment, were not living in Germany. Although the scheme did not expressly specify any nationality requirement, it had the effect of discriminating against non-German nationals who were more likely to have been abroad when they were appointed.

Held The ECJ held that this was capable of breaching Article 7(1) of the Regulation, since the rules, in practice, were more likely to favour German nationals. The Court held that Article 7(1) of Regulation (EEC) 1612/68 prohibits both overt and covert forms of discrimination.

Allué and Coonan v Università degli Studi di Venezia Case 33/88

Under Italian legislation, non-Italian nationals working as language teachers could only enter into fixed term contracts of five years, whereas other university teachers were not subject to such limitations.

Held The ECJ held that this was in breach of Article 39(2) EC (ex 48(2)) and Article 7(1) of Regulation (EEC) 1612/68.

13.4.3 Equality of social and tax advantages – Article 7(2)

Fiorini (née Christini) v Société Nationale des Chemins de Fer Français (SNCF) Case 32/75

F, the Italian widow of an Italian national who had worked in France, applied for a special fare reduction on the French railways, available to large families. Her husband had claimed it whilst he was alive. When she was refused, F brought an action before a French tribunal, which considered that the social and tax advantages, referred to in Article 7(2), were restricted to advantages granted within a work context or because a person was a worker.

Held The ECJ held, in a preliminary ruling from the French tribunal, that Article 7(2) covered all social and tax advantages, whether or not attached to contracts of employment. These rights continued even after the worker's death, since the family had a right to remain in the State under Regulation (EEC) 1251/70. F was entitled to the special fare reduction.

Ministère Public v Even and ONPTS Case 207/78

Even, a French worker in Belgium, received an early retirement pension. However, his pension was less than Belgian nationals in similar circumstances to him.

The ECJ defined social advantages as:

> Those which, whether or not linked to a contract of employment, are generally granted to national workers primarily because of their objective status as workers, or by virtue of the mere fact of their residence in the national territory.

O'Flynn v Adjudication Officer Case C-237/94

O was an Irish national resident in the UK as a former migrant worker. In 1988, his son died and he was buried in Ireland. O applied for a means tested funeral payment. This was refused on the grounds that the burial had not taken place in the UK as required by the relevant regulations. O appealed to the Social Security Appeals Tribunal who dismissed his claim. On appeal, the Court of Appeal sought a preliminary ruling from the ECJ.

Held The ECJ held that the Regulations contravened Article 7(2) of Regulation (EEC) 1612/68. O was entitled to the benefit, although the UK authorities were entitled to limit the payment to an amount fixed by reference to the normal cost of a burial within the UK.

Centre Public d'Aide Sociale de Courcelles v Lebon Case 316/85

In this case, the ECJ held that the rights under Regulation 7(2) do not extend to a person looking for work.

Belgium v Taghavi Case C-243/91

Here, the Iranian wife of an Italian worker working in Belgium was not entitled to an invalidity benefit, because a non-EU spouse of a Belgian national would not have been entitled either. The ECJ made it clear that the social advantage claimed must be a social advantage to nationals of the worker's host state.

13.4.4 Article 7(3): Access to training in vocational schools and retraining centres

R v Inner London Education Authority ex p Hinde (1985)

H, an Irishman, along with D, a French woman, and P, another Irishman, applied for local authority educational maintenance grants in England. H applied in respect of an LLB course, whereas D and P applied for grants for teacher training courses. H was refused and sought judicial review of the local authority decision.

Held A vocational training school within the meaning of Article 7(3) is not restricted to courses for apprentices and school leavers, but can also include training for professions. However, the English High Court held that a university law degree trains lawyers, but not legal practitioners, and is therefore not included.

Note ───

The High Court refused to make an Article 234 EC (ex 177) reference on the grounds that it was not necessary within the *Bulmer v Bollinger* guidelines. See Chapter 5.

───

Does Article 7(3) cover maintenance grants?

The ECJ has considered this issue in the following two cases.

Brown v Secretary of State for Scotland Case 197/86

B, a Franco-British dual national, moved from France to Scotland and worked for Ferranti for eight months prior to taking up his place at Cambridge University to study engineering. His place at university was sponsored by Ferranti. He applied for, and was refused, a maintenance grant. He argued this was in breach of both Articles 7(3) and 7(2), that is, the maintenance grant was a social advantage.

Lair v Universität Hannover Case 39/86

L was a French women who had lived in Germany for over five years. During that time, she had worked off and on, with periods of unemployment and training. In 1984, she started a university course in languages, leading to a vocational qualification. She applied for and was also refused a maintenance grant. Lair advanced the same arguments as Brown, above.

The ECJ delivered both judgments on the same day.

Held The ECJ gave narrow scope to Article 7(3), restricting it to institutions offering sandwich or apprenticeship courses. Neither of the above course could satisfy that test. Turning to Article 7(2), the Court held that maintenance grants could come under Article 7(2), as a social or tax advantage. However, whether a person had a right to the maintenance grant depended upon whether they were a worker. The Court stated:

> Insofar as a worker has entered a Member State for the sole purpose of enjoying, after a very short period of work activity, the benefit of the student assistance system ... it should be observed that such abuses are not covered by the Community provisions in question.

The ECJ allowed Lair's claim as she was a worker, but did not allow Brown's because he had acquired the status of worker exclusively as a result of having been accepted at university.

Note ————————————————————————————————————
Without doubt, this is a policy decision. Member states were very worried that people would enter their territories, take up nominal work in order to obtain educational maintenance grants, as if they were a national.

13.4.5 Housing – Article 9

Commission v Greece Case 305/87
Greek legislation prohibited foreign nationals from owning certain property in certain regions of Greece. This action was brought by the Commission.

Held The ECJ held that the Greek legislation was contrary to Articles 39, 43 and 49 EC (ex 48, 52 and 59).

13.5 Rights of workers' families – Regulation (EEC) 1612/68 extends the scope of Article 39 EC (ex 48) to cover workers' families

Note ————————————————————————————————————
Workers' rights of access to training in vocational schools and retraining centres, under Article 7(3) of Regulation (EEC) 1612/68 should not be confused with the rights of family members to have access to education under Article 12 of Regulation (EEC) 1612/68 or the more general right to move freely throughout the Community to receive services.

13.5.1 The spouse and the position of non-married co-habitees

Diatta v Land Berlin Case 267/83
D, a Senegalese woman, had separated from her husband, a French national living and working in Germany, and intended to get a divorce. She was refused an extension on her residence permit on the grounds that she was no longer a family member.

Held The ECJ held that D had not lost her rights of residence, Article 10 of Council Regulation (EEC) 1612/68 does not imply that a family member must live permanently under the same roof.

Netherlands v Reed Case 59/85
AR, a British woman, was refused a residence permit to live in the Netherlands. She had lived with her partner, a British national working in the Netherlands, for several years. Under Dutch law, a foreigner who has a stable relationship with a Dutch national could be treated as a spouse and obtain a right of residence.

Held The ECJ held that the term spouse contained in Regulation (EEC) 1612/68 applied only to married couples. In her own right, R did not have a right of residence. However, the ECJ considered that the Dutch policy described above must grant the same treatment to a person who has a stable relationship with a worker who is a national of another Member State but is employed in the Netherlands. The Court also considered the issue under Article 7(2) – social and tax advantages – and said that a worker working in another Member State could have an unmarried partner reside with them as a social advantage.

R v Secretary of State for the Home Department ex p Sandhu (1983)

S, an Indian, had married a German woman. In 1975 they both settled in England, each obtaining a five year residence permit. S obtained a steady job. In 1976, they had a son, after which they separated and the wife returned to Germany with the son. In 1980, S was informed that he was no longer entitled to remain in the UK.

Held Initially, the High Court held that S could remain. However, this decision was overruled by both the Court of Appeal and the House of Lords and S was deported. If the EC spouse leaves the UK, then the non-EC spouse loses the dependent right of residence and is not entitled to remain.

R v Immigration Appeal Tribunal and Surinder Singh ex p Secretary of State for the Home Department Case C-370/90

S, was an Indian national who had married a British woman. Both S and his wife had returned to the UK after working and living in Germany for two years. The couple had separated and were granted a decree nisi. The UK authorities tried to deport S when his wife returned to live in Germany. S sought judicial review. The High Court sought a ruling from the ECJ, asking whether the question should be dealt with under national law or Community law.

Held The ECJ held that S should be treated as a spouse of an EC worker (as opposed to a UK national) because of the period of employment in Germany. Accordingly, as the spouse of an EC worker, he was entitled to remain in the UK whilst the marriage still existed.

13.5.2 The worker's dependants

Centre Public d'Aide Sociale de Courcelles v Lebon Case C-316/85

Held The ECJ held that, when a child of a worker reaches the age of 21, unless he or she continues to be a dependent of the worker, the grown-up child will not be covered by Regulation (EEC) 1612/68.

13.5.3 Workers' families have the right to install themselves with the worker – Article 10(3) Regulation (EEC) 1612/68

Commission v Germany (Re Housing) Case 249/86

Under Article 10 of Regulation (EEC) 1612/68, a worker can install himself and his family in a host Member State so long as he can provide accommodation for his family which is 'considered as normal for national workers'. In Germany, the rules implementing this Regulation extended this requirement and the renewal of a residence permit was also conditional upon this accommodation requirement.

Held The ECJ held that the requirement of Article 10(3), which states that a worker must house his family in housing considered as normal for national workers, applies at the time that the worker installs himself in the host State. It is not a continuing requirement.

13.5.4 Family members have the right to take up activity as employed persons – Article 11 of Regulation (EEC) 1612/68

Gül v Regierungs-Präsident Düsseldorf Case 131/85

A Turkish-Cypriot man married an English woman working in Germany. He had qualifications in medicine from the University of Istanbul and in anaesthetics in Germany. He had also worked as an anaesthetist in Germany on a temporary basis for some time. When he applied for permission to practice permanently, he was refused on the grounds of his nationality.

Held The ECJ held that this was a breach of Article 11 of Regulation (EEC) 1612/68.

13.5.5 Family members have the right of access to education – Article 12 Regulation (EEC) 1612/68

Michel S v Fonds National de Réclassement Social des Handicapes Case 76/72

M, was the disabled son of an Italian worker who had worked in Belgium until his death. M applied for various benefits, including a disability benefit designed to enable Belgian nationals to recover their ability to work. He was refused the benefit.

Held The ECJ held that the list of educational arrangements in Article 12 was not exhaustive and could also include disability benefits. Here, the Court gave a generous interpretation to the provisions of Article 12.

Cassagrande v Ländeshauptstadt München Case 9/74

C, the son of an Italian worker living and working in Germany, applied for a grant in respect of attendance at secondary school. Under the German rules the grant was restricted and C was refused.

Held The ECJ held that a worker's child can participate in education on the same terms as a citizen of the host country. This equality is not just confined to access to education. The court clearly stated that Article 12 and the right to access to education extended to any 'general measures intended to facilitate educational attendance'. This included a grant to attend a secondary school in Germany.

Landesamt für Ausbildungsförderung Nordrhein-Westfalen v Gaal Case C-7/94

G, a Belgian, was born 1967 but brought up in Germany from 1969. His father died in 1987 and he was in receipt of an 'orphan's allowance'. He was not financially dependent on his mother. He was studying biology at university in Germany and, in 1989, applied for funds to study for a year at university in the UK. This was refused by the authorities in Germany, as he was over 21 and was not financially dependent on either parent. He appealed.

Held The definition of 'child' for the purposes of Article 12 of Regulation (EEC) 1612/68 was *not* subject to the same conditions as Articles 10(l) and 11 of the Regulation. Therefore, Article 12 may encompass children aged over 21 and no longer dependent. Otherwise, students would be rendered ineligible for State financial assistance as soon as they reached 21 and were financially independent of their parents.

13.6 Article 39 EC (ex 48) does not cover wholly internal measures

R v Saunders Case 175/78

S was charged with theft and bound over. Under the terms of the order, she undertook not to enter England or Wales for three years. She broke her undertaking and was brought before Bristol Crown Court. S sought to challenge the terms of the binding over order on the grounds that it infringed Article 39 EC (ex 48).

Held The provisions of the Treaty on the freedom of movement of workers cannot be applied to situations which are wholly internal to the Member State. There was no factor connecting S to any of the situations envisaged by Community law.

Aubertin and Others Cases C-29, 30, 31, 32, 33, 34 and 35/94

Various French nationals were prosecuted under French law with operating hairdressing salons in France without either a hairdressing diploma or a certificate. The French law was passed in order to implement Directive 82/489/EEC. Not all the Member States regulated hairdressing. The effect of this is that non-French nationals could lawfully operate hairdressing salons in France, without either a hairdressing diploma or a certificate, while French nationals could not. The French nationals appealed, arguing that this amounted to reverse discrimination.

Held As there was no cross-border activity in the case, the ECJ held that EC law had no application.

Möser v Land Baden Württemberg Case 180/83

M, a German national who had always lived in the Federal Republic of Germany, was refused permission to undertake the post-graduate training necessary to become a teacher. The Land refused because of its uncertainty about M's loyalty to the German Constitution, on the basis that M was a long standing and active member of the Communist Party. M contested the decision and argued that it was in breach of Article 39 EC (ex 48) in that it made it impossible for him to become a teacher and would, therefore, be precluded from obtaining teaching posts in other Member States.

Held (ECJ Article 234 EC (ex 177) reference) A purely hypothetical prospect of employment in another Member State does not establish a sufficient connection with Community law to justify the application of Article 39 EC (ex 48). M's argument failed.

Land Nordrhein-Westfalen v Kari Uecker and Vera Jacquet v Land Nordrhein-Westfalen Cases C-64 and 56/96

KU and VJ, respectively Norwegian and Russian nationals, were married to German nationals with whom they lived in Germany. They both challenged their fixed term contracts of employment alleging that they breached Article 11 of Regulation (EEC) 1612/68.

Held The ECJ held that this was not covered by Community law. Since neither of the applicant' partners had exercised their right of free movement, the case was a purely internal matter.

13.7 Derogations from Article 39 EC (ex 48) – limitations on the freedom of movement of workers – Directive 64/221/EEC

13.7.1 Measures taken on public policy or public security grounds must be based exclusively on the personal conduct of the individual concerned

Van Duyn v Home Office Case 41/74

VD, was a Dutch national and a member of the Church of Scientology. She was appointed as Secretary to the UK's branch of the Church, based in England. When VD arrived at Gatwick Airport, she was refused entry. Although she presented proof of her employment, her entry was refused on the grounds that the Home Office had declared as undesirable any person entering the country to work for the Church. However, at that time, the Church was not prohibited and there were no restrictions on UK nationals becoming employees of the Church. VD appealed.

Held In an Article 234 EC (ex 177) preliminary ruling, the ECJ held that Article 3(1) of Directive 64/221/EEC, by providing that measures taken on the grounds of public policy shall be based exclusively on the personal conduct of the individual, is intended to limit the discretionary power of the Member State to prevent entry or expel foreign nationals.

The ECJ held that:

- a person's past association cannot in general justify a decision to refuse entry;
- present association may be taken into account when determining personal conduct;
- it is not necessary for an activity to be unlawful to be against public policy providing that the Member State has taken measures to counteract these activities.

Because the UK Government was taking steps to control the activities of the Church of Scientology, it was able to refuse entry to Ms Van Duyn.

Note ———

In the light of the ECJ's more recent judgments in *R v Bouchereau* Case 30/77 and A*doui and Cornuaille v Belgium* Cases 115 and 116/81, the decision relating to Ms Van Duyn would almost certainly have been different.

Bonsignore v Oberstadtdirektor der Stadt Köln Case 67/74

B, an Italian worker living in Germany, illegally acquired a gun with which he later accidentally shot his brother. He was fined only for unlawful possession of a firearm, but his deportation was ordered. The authorities argued this was necessary to deter other immigrants from committing similar offences, even though they accepted that B was unlikely to commit further offences.

Held The ECJ rejected the argument and held that a person could not be deported as a 'scapegoat' to deter other foreign nationals from committing similar offences. The decision to deport must be based purely on a person's personal conduct and regard should be had of the likely prospects of that person committing further offences.

13.7.2 Public policy and public security: previous criminal convictions do not in themselves constitute grounds

R v Bouchereau Case 30/77

PB, a French national, was convicted of possession of illegal drugs in the UK in January 1976.

Held The existence of a previous criminal conviction can only be taken into account in so far as the circumstances which gave rise to that conviction are evidence of personal conduct constituting a present threat to the requirements of public policy.

R v Home Secretary ex p Marchon (1993)

The English High Court held that a single conviction for importing heroin, with a street value of £500,000, into the UK was of sufficient gravity in itself to constitute a threat to public policy.

Note ──

However, see also the case of *Astrid Proll*, below, 13.9, where serious previous convictions for terrorist activities could not be taken into account.

13.8 Public policy

Ruttili v Minister for the Interior Case 36/75

R was an Italian national living in France. Between 1967 and 1968, he was a political and trade union activist. The French authorities had become increasingly concerned about R and issued a deportation order. This was later altered to a restriction order which effectively required R to stay in certain areas and thus limited his movements within France. In particular, R was not allowed to reside in the province where his family were living. R challenged the order on the grounds that it breached his free movement as a worker.

Held The ECJ held that the right of the authorities of the Member States to restrict the movement of workers on the grounds of public policy had to be restrictively interpreted. They would only be legal if the restrictions were not discriminatory (that is, applied also to a Member State's own nationals). Restrictions could only be justified if the person's presence constituted a 'genuine and serious threat to public policy'.

A Member State can invoke the public policy exception to refuse entry or to deport a person to the whole of the territory, but it cannot use it to restrict movement within its territory. Such a restriction would constitute discriminatory treatment between nationals and non-nationals.

R v Bouchereau Case 30/77

For facts, see above, 13.7.2.

Held The ECJ held that there must be 'a genuine and serious threat to the requirements of public policy affecting one of the fundamental interests of society'.

Adoui and Cornuaille v Belgium Cases 115 and 116/81

A and C were French women refused a residence permit by the Belgian authorities on the grounds that their conduct was considered to be contrary to public policy, because they were 'waitresses in a bar which was suspect from the point of view of morals'.

Held The ECJ held that the refusal could only be justified on public policy grounds if Belgian nationals were subject to the same measures. The Court held that the refusal was discriminatory because the Belgian authorities had not adopted repressive measures or other genuine and effective measures intended to combat the same conduct on the part of it's own nationals.

Note ——————————————————————————————

Thus, a Member State must show that a person's present personal conduct represents a genuine and serious threat to one of the fundamental interests of society, and that the State is engaging in repressive or effective measures to combat such conduct amongst its own nationals. Contrast this with the earlier decision in the *Van Duyn* case, above, 13.7.1.

Criminal proceedings against Donatella Calfa Case C-348/96

Ms Calfa, an Italian national on holiday in Greece, was convicted by a Greek criminal court and sentenced to three months' imprisonment for a drugs offence. Under Greek law, non-Greek nationals convicted of drugs offences were automatically expelled from Greece for life. Ms Calfa appealed to the Greek Supreme Court which sought a preliminary ruling, asking whether the Greek legislation was compatible with Articles 39, 43 and 49 (ex 48, 52 and 59).

Held The ECJ held that criminal law may not restrict the freedoms guaranteed by the Treaty and that life expulsion was contrary to Community law. The Court did accept that the use of drugs represents a threat, which justifies special measures against foreigners. Nevertheless, the public policy exception must be interpreted restrictively and criminal convictions alone are not sufficient grounds to justify expulsion.

13.9 Public security

Astrid Proll v Entry Clearance Officer, Düsseldorf (1988)

AP, a German who had been a member of the Baader-Meinhoff terrorist group, was convicted for a variety of offences in Germany in 1989. However, the German court, accepting that AP had reformed, sentenced her to a minimum of 12 months. In 1980, 1981 and then, in 1985, AP applied for permission to enter the UK, in the last instance to work as a photographer. On each occasion, she was refused entry. In 1985 she appealed to the Immigration Appeal Tribunal.

Held The Immigration Appeal Tribunal held that her previous crimes were no justification for refusing her entry, as she did not pose a present threat to either public security or public policy. She was allowed to enter as a worker.

13.10 Public health

Commission v Netherlands Case C-68/89

The Commission brought this action against the Netherlands in respect of a number of the formalities, including certain health checks, carried out by the Dutch authorities when non-Dutch EC nationals were seeking entry into the Netherlands as workers.

Held The ECJ held that a Member State cannot carry out routine medical checks on other EC nationals exercising their rights under the free movement provisions. It also held that a Member State cannot require those persons to provide medical evidence that they do not suffer from any prescribed diseases. However, a Member State can carry out medical examinations where they have reason to believe that a person has obvious symptoms of any of the prescribed diseases.

13.11 Article 39(4) EC (ex 48(4)) – employment in the public service

Sotgiu v Deutsche Bundespost Case 152/73

For facts, see above, 13.4.2. The German Post Office argued that the provisions of Article 39 EC (ex 48) did not apply since Sotgiu was employed in the public service.

Held The ECJ held that Article 39(4) EC (ex 48(4)) does not apply to all employment in the public service, only 'certain activities' involving the exercise of official authority. Article 39(4) EC (ex 48(4)) must be interpreted restrictively and cannot be used to justify discriminatory measures with regard to pay or other conditions of employment.

Commission v Belgium (Re Public Employees) Case 149/79

Belgian local authorities and public bodies made it a condition of service that a worker be of Belgian nationality. This applied to all posts, including unskilled jobs, such as janitors. The Commission brought Article 226 EC (ex 169) proceedings.

Held The ECJ held that Article 39(4) EC (ex 48(4)) should only apply to those positions which require a specific bond of allegiance to the State. Such posts must involve the exercise of powers conferred by public law and duties which involve safeguarding the general interests of the State.

Commission v France (Re French Nurses) Case 307/84 [1986] ECR 1725
Held Nurses were held not to be in the public service for the purposes of Article 48(4).

Allué and Coonan Case 33/88
Held University teachers were held not to be in the public service for the purposes of Article 39(4) EC (ex 48(4)).

Commission v Luxembourg (Re Public Service Employees) Case C-473/93
Luxembourg law banned non nationals from a wide range of activities in the public utilities (gas and electricity), public education, health care and transport. The Luxembourg Government argued, by way of defence, that its tiny population, coupled with the attractiveness of working for the Luxembourg civil service/public sector, would lead to an influx of workers from abroad.

Held The ECJ held that Article 39(4) EC (ex 48(4)) did not authorise a Member State to 'unilaterally exclude workers from other Member States from entire areas of occupational activity'.

13.12 Procedural safeguards – Directive 64/221/EEC

13.12.1 The duty to give reasons when entry into a Member State is refused

R v Secretary of State for Home Affairs ex p Dannenberg (1984)
A deportation order was made against D by a magistrates' court. This was challenged by D.

Held A worker must be informed of the grounds on which entry or residence is refused, unless this would be contrary to the interests of public security. The deportation order was quashed.

13.12.2 Remedies – Article 9 – workers are entitled to the same legal remedies as are available to nationals.

R v Secretary of State for the Home Department Case ex p Santillo Case 131/79
MS, an Italian, was convicted in the UK of various violent crimes including rape, buggery and indecent assault. He was sentenced to eight years with a judicial recommendation that the prison sentence be followed by deportation. Five years later, the Home Office issued a deportation order.

Held The ECJ held that it was essential that the social danger resulting from a foreigner's presence should be addressed at the time when the decision to deport is made, because a person's conduct may have changed over time.

14 Freedom of Establishment – Articles 43–48 EC (ex 52–58); Freedom to Provide or Receive Services – Articles 49–55 EC (ex 59–66)

14.1 The nature of establishment

Commission v Germany (Re Insurance Services) Case 205/84

German law required that providers of insurance services be both authorised by the German authorities and also be established in Germany. This had the effect of making it more difficult for non-German insurance companies to provide a service in Germany.

Held Although the case was concerned with the provision of services, rather than establishment, the ECJ held that the long term establishment of offices in the host Member State, which are staffed by a company's employees, should be regarded as establishment, even where the legal entity remains in the home State.

Gebhard v Consiglio dell'Ordine degli Avvocati e Procuratori di Milano Case C55/94

Gebhard was a German national and a member of the Stuttgart Bar. He had resided in Italy since 1978, where he had practices in set of chambers in Milan. In 1989, he opened his own chambers and began using the title 'avvocato'. Following complaints from a number of Italian lawyers, the Milan Bar Council banned Gebhard from using the title on the basis that it was reserved for lawyers possessing Italian legal and professional qualifications who were members of the Italian Bar Association. Directive 77/249/EEC, which permitted lawyers to provide temporary services in another Member State, did not permit the establishment of either chambers or a principal office in another Member State. The Italian court asked the ECJ to give a preliminary ruling on, *inter alia*, the distinction between establishment and services.

Held The ECJ held:

... the fact that the provision of services is temporary does not mean that the provider of services within the meaning of the Treaty may not equip himself with some form of infrastructure within the host Member State (including an office, chambers or consulting rooms) insofar as such infrastructure is necessary for the purposes of performing the services in question. Services are characterised by their temporary nature and also by issues such as regularity, periodicity and continuity.

The ECJ also stated, that 'establishment' involves, in the case of professionals setting up a second professional base, a 'stable and continuous basis ... contributing to economic and social inter-penetration within the Community'.

On the facts, the ECJ decided that Gebhard was seeking to establish himself.

Note ————
The ECJ was also asked to consider the compatability of the Italian Bar Association rules with the Treaty. This is considered more fully below.

TV 10 SA v Commissariaat voor de Media Case C-23/93

TV 10 was a cable television broadcasting company, incorporated in Luxembourg, but whose broadcasts were clearly designed and intended for the Dutch market. The company was refused access to the Dutch cable network. It appeared that TV 10 set up their operations in Luxembourg in order to avoid Dutch laws on broadcasting.

Held The ECJ held that where an enterprise is situated in one Member State, but its activities are directed entirely or mainly towards another Member State (often in order to avoid more stringent rules and regulations applying in the latter), then the enterprise will be deemed to be established there.

Note ————
The Court also held that Articles 49 and 50 EC (ex 59 and 60) applied to cable broadcasts transmitted by cable operators established in one Member State but supplied by a broadcaster in another, even if the latter established itself there in order to avoid legislation applicable to domestic broadcasters.

Steinhauser v City of Biarritz Case 197/84

S, a German, lived in the city of Biarritz. He was a professional artist and wished to rent a hut to exhibit his work but was refused on the grounds of his nationality.

Held The ECJ held that the freedom of establishment provided for in Article 43 EC (ex 52) was not confined to the taking-up of an activity as a self-employed person, but also extended to the pursuit of that activity in its widest sense.

14.2   The nature of services

See previous comments on services in *Gebhard*, above, 14.1.

Alpine Investments BV v Minister van Financiën Case C-384/93

Alpine Investments, a company established in the Netherlands, offered a brokerage service. They received orders from clients relating to investments on commodities futures markets and passed them on for execution to other brokers throughout the EU. Their business was largely conducted on the telephone. The company challenged a Dutch law which prohibited companies from approaching prospective clients over the telephone (known as coldcalling). They argued this was an infringement of their right to provide services to potential clients outside the Netherlands.

Held The ECJ held that Article 49 EC (ex 59) also covers situations where a service is provided or received without the provider or recipient leaving their own Member State. Thus, the application of Article 49 EC (ex 59) does not depend on prior relations between the provider of the service and the recipient and there is no need for the service provider to leave their home State.

Note
This case is considered more fully below, 14.7.

14.3   Articles 43 and 49 EC (ex 52 and 59) are binding on the State and all its emanations and recognised professional bodies

Walrave and Koch v Association Union Cycliste Internationale Case 36/74

W and K, both Dutch nationals, provided professional services as pacemakers on cycle races. Under World Championship Cycling rules, the pacemaker was required to be of the same nationality as the cyclist participating in the race. W and K challenged these rules as being incompatible with Article 49 EC (ex 59).

Held The ECJ held that the provisions of Article 49 EC (ex 59) are to be dealt with in a similar fashion to those in Article 39 EC (ex 48):

The activities referred to in Article 59 [now 49 EC] are not to be distinguished by their nature from those in Article 48 [now 39 EC], but only by the fact that they are performed outside the ties of the contract of employment.

14.4 Direct effect of Articles 43 and 49 EC (ex 52 and 59)

Reyners v Belgium Case 2/74

R was a Dutchman but was born, educated and resided in Belgium, and was also a doctor of Belgian law. However, he was refused admission to the Belgian Bar on the grounds that he was not a Belgian national. R challenged this decision on the basis that this was a breach of his rights under Article 43 EC (ex 52). The Belgian authorities argued against the direct effect of Article 43 EC (ex 52) maintaining that the effect of Article 43 EC (ex 52) was dependent upon the adoption of Directives under Article 47 EC (ex 57) (dealing with the mutual recognition of qualifications).

Held On a reference to the ECJ, it was held that Article 43 EC (ex 52) had to be interpreted in the light of the whole of the EEC Treaty, including Article 12 EC (ex 6), which prohibits any discrimination on the grounds of nationality. Article 43 EC (ex 52) was directly effective at the end of the transitional period and the provisions of Article 43 EC (ex 52) were not dependant upon the adoption of Directives under Article 47 EC (ex 57). The Directives were simply a means of facilitating free movement and not the means of establishing it.

Van Binsbergen v Bestuur van de Bedrijfsvereniging voor de Metaalnijverheid Case 33/74

VB was involved in a social security claim and was represented by K, his legal adviser. During the proceedings, K moved from the Netherlands to Belgium. According to Dutch rules, K was no longer entitled to represent his client because he was not habitually resident in the Netherlands. K argued that the residency requirement under Dutch law restricted his rights under Article 49 EC (ex 59) to supply services.

Held The ECJ held, on a reference, that Article 49(1) EC (ex 59(1)) was directly effective and not subject to any residence requirement. The court also held that the effect of the Articles were not dependent upon the adoption of any Directives dealing with the specific professions.

(This case is considered more fully below in respect of the residency requirement, see 14.6.2.)

Walrave and Koch v Association Union Cycliste Internationale Case 36/74

For facts, see above, 14.3.

Held The ECJ held that the provisions of Article 49 EC (ex 59) are to be dealt with in a similar fashion to those in Article 39 EC (ex 48):

> The activities referred to in Article 59 [now 49 EC] are not to be distinguished by their nature from those in Article 48 [now 39 EC], but only by the fact that they are performed outside the ties of the contract of employment.

14.5 Articles 43 and 49 EC (ex 52 and 59) and the prohibition against discrimination

Procureur du Roi v Royer Case 48/75

R was a French national living in Belgium. He was ordered to leave Belgium by the Belgian police on the grounds that he had not complied with all the administrative formalities when he entered Belgium.

Held On a reference from a national court which was uncertain as to whether the proceedings fell under the freedom of movement of workers provisions (Article 39 EC (ex 48)) or establishment (Article 43 EC (ex 52)) or services (Article 49 EC (ex 59)), the ECJ held that:

> ... comparison of these different provisions shows that they are based on the same principles, both in so far as they concern the entry into and residence in the territory of Member States of persons covered by Community law and the prohibition of all discrimination between them on the grounds of nationality.

Commission v Italy (Re Housing Aid) Case 63/86

This case concerned cheap mortgage facilities which were only available to Italian nationals. The Commission brought an action under Article 226 EC (ex 169).

Held This was in breach of Article 12 EC (ex 6). Nationals of a Member State who wish to pursue an activity as a self-employed person in another Member State must be able to obtain housing in conditions equivalent to those enjoyed by the nationals of the host Member State. Accordingly, mortgage facilities should be available to EC nationals providing a service in Italy.

Ministère Public v Van Wesemael Cases 110 and 111/78

VW, a Belgian, was prosecuted in Belgium for using the services of a French employment agency and not one registered in Belgium.

Held The ECJ held on a reference that, since the French agency was registered in France, it was contrary to Article 49 EC (ex 59) for another State (that is, Belgium) to restrict its right to provide services in that country,

14.6 Under the same conditions

- The freedom of establishment for a self-employed person or business is exercisable 'under the same conditions laid down for its own nationals by the laws of the country where such establishment is effected' (Article 43 EC (ex 52)).

- A person may provide services in another Member State 'under the same conditions as are imposed by that State on its own nationals'. (Article 50 EC (ex 60)).

These requirements have implications in relation to the recognition of qualifications and professional rules of conduct.

14.6.1 The recognition of qualifications

Situation where no harmonising Directive exists

Thieffry v Conseil de l'Ordre des Avocats à la Cour de Paris Case 71/76

T was a Belgian national with a Belgian law degree which had been recognised by the University of Paris. T had also passed the qualifying certificate in France for the profession of *avocat*. However, the French Bar Council refused to allow T to undertake the practical training necessary for the French Bar.

Held The French Bar Council could not refuse this permission because his qualifications had been recognised as being equivalent to those required in France.

Patrick v Ministre des Affaires Culturelles Case 11/77

P was an English architect but was refused permission to practice as an architect in France.

Held He was entitled to rely on the provisions of Articles 43 and 12 EC (ex 52 and 7). Although there was no Directive relating to the architects' profession at that time, the English qualification had been recognised as equivalent to the French qualification by a French ministerial decree in 1964.

Vlassopoulou v Ministerium für Justiz, Bundes und Europaangelegenheiten Baden-Württemberg Case C-340/89

V was a Greek national who had a Greek law degree and had been admitted to the Athens Bar. She also had experience in professional practice in Germany and in German law. However, she was refused admission to the German Bar and authorisation to practice because it was argued that she lacked the necessary German qualifications.

Held The ECJ held, on a reference from the German courts, that where a person requests to be admitted to a profession, to which access under national law depends upon the possession of a diploma or a professional qualification, the Member State concerned must:

> ...take into consideration the diplomas, certificates and other evidence of qualifications which the person concerned has acquired, in order to exercise the same profession in another Member State, by making a comparison between the specialised knowledge and abilities certified by those diplomas and the knowledge and qualifications required by the national rules.

Ministère Public v Auer (No I) Case 136/78

A, an Austrian, qualified as a vet whilst in Italy, but practised in France, where he took up French citizenship. French law required him to take a competency test because the French authorities did not recognise the Italian qualification as equivalent to the French. A repeatedly failed the test. He argued that he was qualified already and that the tests were, therefore, excessive. However, as the period for implementation of the relevant harmonising Directive (78/1026/EEC) had not yet expired, his entitlement to practice remained governed by French law. The position changed when the deadline for the implementation of the Veterinary Surgeons' Directive was passed; his Italian qualification had to be recognised. (See *Auer (No 2)* Case 271/82.)

Effect of mutual recognition or harmonising of qualifications Directives

Broekmeulen v Huisarts Registratie Commissie Case 246/80

B had qualified as a GP in Belgium and wished to practise in Holland. In Holland, GPs were required to undertake three years' specialised training but this was not necessary in Belgium. Directive 75/362/EEC did not require GPs to undertake further training additional to the original qualification and B's qualification was recognised in Article 3 of the Directive.

Held On a reference, it was held by the ECJ that the Dutch General Practitioners' Committee could not refuse B permission to practice as a GP in Holland.

Knoors v Secretary of State for Economic Affairs Case 115/78

K, a Dutch national, was a plumber in Belgium. However, he was not allowed to practise as a plumber in the Netherlands. A harmonising Directive did exist (64/427/EEC) which covered trades such as plumbing. Nevertheless, the Dutch authorities argued that K could not rely on the provisions of the Directive because he was a Dutch person seeking to establish himself in the Netherlands!

Held The ECJ held that K could benefit from the provisions of the Directive. The right of freedom of movement and establishment is conferred on the nationals of all Member States. Although the free movement provisions cannot be applied to purely internal measures (see *R v Saunders*, Chapter 13), Article 43 EC (ex 52) covers situations such as in the facts of this case.

14.6.2 Professional rules of conduct

Residency requirements

Van Binsbergen v Bestuur van de Bedrijfsvereniging voor de Metaalnijverheid Case 33/74

For facts, see above, 14.4.

Held The ECJ held that:

... taking into account the particular nature of the service to be provided, specific requirements imposed on the person providing the service cannot be considered incompatible with the Treaty where they have as their purpose the application of professional rules justified by the general good – in particular, rules relating to organisation, qualification, professional ethics, supervision and liability which are binding upon any person established in the State in which the services are provided.

Coenen v Sociaal-Economische Raad Case 39/75

A Dutch national, living in Belgium, worked as an insurance broker over the border in Holland. Dutch law required brokers to live in Holland.

The ECJ accepted the residence requirement in principle, but stated that it should be subject to the test of proportionality – was it the least restrictive way of regulating the profession?

Held The ECJ held that having a place of business in the Netherlands was sufficient. It was not necessary for brokers to live there as well. The Court also stated of residency rules that they must be non-discriminatory, justified in the interest of the public and proportionate.

Commission v Luxembourg Case C-351/90

Luxembourg operated a so called 'single surgery' rule which prevented GPs established in another Member State from operating a surgery in Luxembourg, purportedly to ensure proximity between GPs and patients.

Held The ECJ held this to be unjustified. A general restriction was 'unduly restrictive' and 'too absolute and too general'.

Licensing or registration requirements

Webb Case 279/80

Criminal proceedings were brought against Webb for running a manpower agency which was established in the UK and recruited workers to work on a temporary basis in the Netherlands. Webb had a licence in the UK, but not from the Dutch authorities. He was prosecuted for not having a licence and for supplying workers in this fashion.

The ECJ was asked to provide a preliminary ruling on compatibility of the licence requirement with Article 49 EC (ex 59).

Held The ECJ held that, when a host Member State applies its own rules, it must also consider the effect of the national professional rules of the home Member State, upon the conduct of the applicant, in order to determine whether its own rules are justified. Duplication of rules will not be justified.

14.7 The development of a rule of reason in relation to establishment and services

In the following cases, we see the ECJ developing a set of criteria against which national rules will be considered to determine their compatibility with Articles 43 and 49 EC (ex 52 and 59). These criteria are very similar to the 'rule of reason' developed in the *Cassis de Dijon* case (Case 120/78) (see Chapter 12).

Van Binsbergen v Bestuur van de Bedrijfsvereniging voor de Metaalnijverheid Case 33/74

For facts, see above, 14.4.

Therefore, the Court held that a residency requirement may be compatible with Articles 49 and 50 EC (ex 59 and 60) where the requirement is objectively justified by the need to ensure compliance with professional rules of conduct.

Commission v Germany (Re Insurance Services) Case 205/84

In a series of cases (listed below), the Commission challenged four Member States in respect of their rules on the provision of insurance services, on the basis that the rules breached Articles 49 and 50 EC (ex 59 and 60). The Member States typically required the providers of insurance services to be established in the host State and authorised to practice there. The German authorities argued that this enabled them to monitor insurance firms and protect German policy holders.

Held The ECJ held that these Articles require the removal not only of all discrimination against providers of a service on the basis of nationality, but also all restrictions on his freedom to provide services imposed, by reason of the fact that he is established in another Member State other than that in which the service is to be provided. However, the Court went on to say that that legislation which applied to those engaged in permanent activities could only be applied to those whose activities were merely temporary if the following criteria were satisfied:

- there were imperative reasons relating to the public interest;
- the public interest requirement was not already protected by the rules of the originating State; and
- the same result cannot be achieved by less restrictive means.

Applying these criteria, the Court found that the establishment requirement was not justified. The authorisation requirement, on the other hand, could be upheld for the protection of policy holders and insured persons.

Note ————————————————————————————————————

See, also:

- *Commission v France* Case 220/83;
- *Commission v Denmark* Case 252/83;
- *Commission v Ireland* Case 206/84.

Sager v Dennemeyer & Co Case C-76/90

D, a specialist patent renewal company based in the UK, provided services in Germany. They did so without a licence required under German law for any persons attending to the legal affairs of others. S, a German patent renewal company, challenged D. D argued that the German licence was in breach of Article 49 EC (ex 59).

Held The ECJ, on a preliminary ruling, held that the freedom to provide services may only be limited by rules which:

- are justified by imperative reasons relating to the public interest; and

- apply to all persons and undertakings pursuing an activity in the host State in so far as that interest is not protected by rules in the State in which the service provider is established; and

- are objectively necessary in order to ensure compliance with professional rules and must not exceed what is necessary to obtain those public interest objectives.

Customs and Excise Commissioner v Schindler Case 275/92

S were responsible for organising lotteries in West Germany. They sent invitations to participate in the German National Lottery to the UK. These were confiscated by the UK customs authorities on the grounds that they were in breach of the Revenue Act 1898 and the Lotteries and Amusements Act 1976, which prohibited the importation of adverts or other notices relating to lotteries for publication in the UK. S argued that these provisions were in breach of Article 28 EC (ex 30), or alternatively Article 49 EC (ex 59), since they prohibited the importation of tickets relating to a lottery lawfully conducted in another Member State.

Held The Divisional Court referred the matter to the ECJ, who held that, although the tickets were not 'goods' within Article 28 EC (ex 30), there was a *prima facie* infringement of Article 49 EC (ex 59), because the freedom to provide the service (participation in a lottery) was being restricted. The fact that the UK legislation applied without discrimination to all large scale lotteries, whatever their place of origin, was irrelevant. However, on the facts, the UK legislation was justified. The objectives of the UK legislation were various: to prevent crime and fraud; to avoid stimulating demand in the gambling sector; to ensure that lotteries could not be operated for personal or commercial profit, but solely for charitable, sporting or cultural purposes. Consequently, the UK legislation, being more concerned with the protection of the recipients of services and consumers in general than discrimination on national grounds, did not infringe Article 49 EC (ex 59).

Alpine Investments BV v Minister van Financien Case C-384/93

Alpine Investments, a company established in the Netherlands, offered a brokerage service. They received orders from clients relating to investments on commodities futures markets and passed them on for execution to other brokers throughout the EU. Their business was largely conducted on the telephone. The company challenged a Dutch law which prohibited companies from approaching prospective clients over the telephone (known as coldcalling). They argued that his was an infringement of their right to provide services to potential clients outside the Netherlands.

Held The ECJ held that the Dutch law was *prima facie* contrary to Article 49 EC (ex 59), but was justified because it was introduced for imperative reasons of public interest. These reasons included maintaining the good reputation of the national financial sector and ensuring the trustworthiness and competence of financial intermediaries. The ban on coldcalling was not disproportionate because there were other methods of approaching clients.

Note
The cases considered above all related to the provision of services under Article 49 EC (ex 59). However, the following case makes it clear that the reasoning also applies to rules which impede the freedom of establishment.

Gebhard v Consiglio dell'Ordine degli Avvocati e Procuratori di Milano Case C-55/94

For the facts, see above, 14.1.

The ECJ was asked to consider the compatibility of the Italian rules with Article 43 EC (ex 52) (since the Court had decided that Gebhard was established in Italy).

Held: National measures which hinder or make less attractive the exercise of the fundamental freedoms guaranteed by the Treaty must fulfil four conditions:

- they must be applied in a non-discriminatory manner;
- they must be justified by imperative requirements in the general interest;
- they must be suitable for the attainment of the objective which they pursue;
- they must not go beyond what is necessary in order to attain that objective.

The Court also stated that Member States must take into account the equivalence of diplomas and, if necessary, proceed to a comparison of the knowledge and qualifications required by their national rules and those of the person concerned.

Note ───

The ECJ, in this case, refers to measures which hinder or make less attractive the exercise of the fundamental freedoms. The case concerned the freedom of establishment, but the wording used by the Court suggests that the Court may be referring to all the fundamental freedoms. What is clear is the fact that the Court seems to have established, in relation to both establishment and services, a rule of reason on similar grounds to the *Cassis de Dijon* rule of reason in relation to goods. The difference here is that the Court refers to imperative requirements in the general interest, rather than mandatory requirements, but the meaning is the same. Also, the Court does not list these 'imperative requirements' like it chose to in the *Cassis* case. However, note the following case, where the Court at least lists some examples.

Syndesmos Ton En Elladi Touristikon Kai Taxidiotikon Grraffeion Ypourgos Ergasias Case C-398/95

The Greek Ministry of Labour adopted legislation which required that licensed tourist guides, who agreed to run tourist programmes organised by Greek or foreign companies, had to be bound by an employment relationship and, consequently, Greek employment legislation. The Greek authorities argued that the rules were necessary to maintain industrial peace as a means of bringing a collective labour agreement to an end and thereby preventing any adverse effects on the economy.

Held The ECJ held that, in forcing an employment relationship onto licensed guides, the Greek legislation could deprive a tourist guide from another Member State of the possibility of working in Greece as a self-employed person and, as such, was a breach of Article 49 EC (ex 159). The Court was not willing to accept the Greek Government's arguments as an overriding public interest. However, the Court made it clear that:

The Court has previously held that compelling grounds of public interest include [for example]:

- protection of workers (*Webb* Case 279/80);
- protection of consumers (*Commission v Germany* Case 205/84 and *Commission v France* Case 220/83);
- the maintenance of national historical and cultural heritage (*Commission v Italy* Case C-180/89);
- the proper appreciation of the artistic and archaeological heritage and the widest possible dissemination of knowledge of the artistic and cultural heritage of a country (*Commission v France* Case C-154/89).

14.8 Limitations on the freedom of establishment and services

Activities concerned with the exercise of official authority (Article 45 EC (ex 55))

Reyners v Belgium State Case 2/74
For facts, see above, 14.4.

The Belgian Government sought to justify the rules of the Belgian Bar on the grounds that the profession of *avocat* fell within the provisions of Article 45 EC (ex 55) – that the profession involved the exercise of official authority.

Held Article 45 EC (ex 55) applied only to 'activities' connected with the exercise of official authority and it did not apply to professions or occupations as a whole.

A Thijssen v Controladienst voor de Verzekeringen Case C-42/92
Held The post of approved commissioner, which involved assisting the Belgian *Office de Contrôle des Assurances* in an auxiliary and preparatory role, did not involve the necessary 'direct and specific participation in the exercise of official authority'. Accordingly, the post could not be limited to Belgian nationals.

Limitations on the grounds of public policy, security and health

Society for the Protection of Unborn Children v Grogan Case C-159/90
The SPUC obtained an injunction from the Irish High Court to prevent student bodies in Ireland distributing information about abortion services in other Member States. The information was found to contravene provisions in the Irish Constitution which upheld the right to life of the unborn child. G (an officer of the student organisation) argued, in their appeal against the injunction, that the Irish law imposed a restriction on the right to provide abortion services and was, therefore, in breach of Articles 49 and 50 EC (ex 59 and 60).

Held The ECJ held that the provision of abortion services for money was a service within the meaning of Article 50 EC (ex 60). However, it held that the link between the information provided by the defendant and the economic service was too tenuous to be regarded as a restriction on the freedom to provide services within the meaning of Article 49 EC (ex 59). There was, therefore, no breach of EC law in the serving of the injunction.

Although the ECJ did not deal specifically with this point, Advocate General Van Gerven was of the opinion that, whilst there was a *prima facie* breach of Article 49 EC (ex 59), the breach was justifiable on the basis that publication of the information would constitute a 'threat to one of the requirements of public policy affecting one of the fundamental interests of society'.

R v HM Treasury ex p Daily Mail and General Trust plc Case 81/87
DMGT plc, a UK company, opened an investment management office in the Netherlands to gain a tax advantage. According to UK law, Treasury

consent was required where a company seeks to transfer its central management and control out of the UK, whilst maintaining its legal personality as a company in the UK. These rules were challenged by means of judicial review.

Held Although the freedom of establishment was a fundamental right in the absence of Community Directives governing this issue, Articles 43 and 48 EC (ex 52 and 58) conferred no right on a company, incorporated under the legislation of a Member State and having its registered office there, to transfer its central management and control to another Member State.

Commission v France, Italy and Greece Cases C-154/89, 180/89 and 198/89

The three Member States each had a requirement that all tourist guides sit an examination in order to become licensed. The Member States argued that this was necessary to ensure that tourist guides provided accurate artistic and cultural information.

Held The ECJ held that this was a restriction on the right to provide services. Whilst it was justifiable on grounds of public policy, it was not justified because a blanket requirement was disproportionate, particularly for popular resorts.

14.9 Freedom to receive services

Luisi and Carbone v Ministero del Tesoro Cases 286/82 and 26/83

Criminal proceedings were brought against L and C in the Italian court on the grounds that the defendants had taken more currency out of the country than the legal limit. The money had been taken out for the purposes of tourism and receiving medical treatment.

Held On a reference to the ECJ, it was held that the money was intended to be payment for services. The freedom to provide services laid down in Article 49 EC (ex 59) also covers the freedom to move freely throughout the Community to receive services in other Member States. Tourists, persons receiving medical treatment, and persons travelling for the purposes of education and business were held to be recipients of services. Therefore, L and C were entitled as recipients of services to take money out of Italy to receive services.

Cowan v Le Trésor Public Case 186/87

C, an Englishman on holiday in Paris, was injured in a mugging. He sought compensation for his injuries in the French courts but was refused access to the French Criminal Injuries Compensation Fund which was only available to French nationals.

Held The ECJ held that, as a recipient of services, C was entitled to make a claim against the compensation fund. This right was held to be a 'corollary' of his right to receive services.

Belgian State v Humbel Case 236/86

For facts, see above, 14.10.

The ECJ held that there is a distinction to be drawn between private services and those available publicly. The ECJ confirmed that Article 50(1) EC (ex 60(1)) applies only to services provided for remuneration. This principle was affirmed in *Wirth v Landeshaupt Hannover* Case C-109/92.

14.10 Right to receive educational and vocational training

Gravier v City of Liège Case 293/83

G was a French woman accepted as a student at the Liège Academy of Arts to do a four year course in strip cartoons. The Academy charged her a special additional fee, known as a *minerval*, because she was a foreign student. Belgian nationals and other EC nationals working in Belgium were not subject to this charge. G challenged the imposition of the *minerval* charge in the Belgian courts.

Held On a reference by the ECJ, access to vocational training was held to be a matter covered by the Treaty, Article 12 EC (ex 6) of which prohibits any discrimination on the grounds of nationality in relation to matters within the scope of the Treaty. The *minerval* was discriminatory and, therefore, in breach of Article 12 EC (ex 6) . The Court defined vocational training very widely and held it to include all forms of teaching which prepares for and leads directly to a particular profession, trade or employment.

Blaizot v University of Liège Case 24/86

B sought reimbursement of the *minerval* charged for a university course in veterinary science.

Held The ECJ held that university education could constitute vocational training.

Belgian State v Humbel Case 236/86

H was the son of a French national living in Luxembourg. The Belgian authorities claimed that H should pay a *minerval* in respect of one year of secondary education he received in Belgium.

Held The ECJ held that, although the one year course was part of a course of general education, it was still to be treated as being vocational if it formed an integral part of an overall programme of vocational education.

Note ————————————————————————————————

Position regarding maintenance grants: see *Brown* Case 197/86 and *Lair* Case 39/86, Chapter 13.

15 Sex Discrimination

15.1 Article 141 EC (ex 119) – equal pay for equal work

15.1.1 Article 141 EC (ex 119) is directly effective – vertically and horizontally

Defrenne v SA Belge de Navigation Aérienne (SABENA) (No 2) Case 43/75
D, an air stewardess, brought a claim against her employer, the Belgian national airline, for damages equivalent to the difference between the pay she received during employment and the comparable rate for her male colleagues who performed the same duties as cabin stewards. The Belgian court referred the matter to the ECJ.

Held Article 141 EC (ex 119) was directly effective. However, the ECJ recognised that such a decision might, in many branches of economic life, result in many claims, which undertakings could not have foreseen, dating back to the time at which such effect came into existence. This might seriously affect the financial situation of many undertakings and even drive some of them to bankruptcy. Therefore, the direct effect of Article 141 EC (ex 119) could not be relied on in order to support claims concerning pay periods prior to the date of judgment, except as regards those workers who had already brought legal proceedings.

15.2 The scope of Article 141 EC (ex 119) – equal pay

15.2.1 Article 141 EC (ex 119) applies to remuneration paid after employment has ceased

Garland v British Rail Engineering Ltd Case 12/81
British Rail's engineering division awarded special travel facilities to male ex-workers *after retirement*. G challenged this policy, on the ground that former female workers, like herself, had no such entitlements. One question was whether the facilities amounted to 'pay'. The House of Lords referred the matter to the ECJ.

Held The facilities were 'pay' within Article 141 EC (ex 119). It was irrelevant that the award was made after termination of employment, as was the fact that it was not actually provided for in the worker's contract of employment.

15.2.2 Statutory social security schemes outside of Article 141 EC (ex 119)

Defrenne v Belgium (No 1) Case 80/70

D, an air hostess, challenged a Belgian law requiring different contribution rates made by employers in the civil aviation industry, in respect of male and female employees, to a statutory social security scheme.

Held She was unsuccessful. A retirement pension established within the framework of a social security scheme laid down by legislation does *not* constitute consideration which the worker receives indirectly in respect of employment from their employer within the meaning of Article 141 EC (ex 119).

15.2.3 Pension contributions are included in Article 141 EC (ex 119)

Bilka-Kaufhaus GmbH v Weber von Hartz Case 170/84

Under BK's non-contributory occupational pension scheme, part time workers were only entitled to join the employers' pension scheme if they had worked for the employer for at least 15 out of the last 20 years. No such limitation was placed on full time staff. WH challenged this scheme, alleging indirect discrimination, as the majority of part time workers were women.

Held The scheme was capable of falling under Article 141 EC (ex 119), as the pension contributions constituted consideration paid by an employer to the employees in respect of employment.

15.2.4 Occupational pension scheme benefits are pay within Article 141 EC (ex 119)

Barber v Guardian Royal Exchange Assurance Group Case C-262/88

B was made redundant at the age of 52 but was denied an early retirement pension under his employer's non-contributory contracted-out pension scheme. Such a pension was only available to men made redundant after their 55th birthday, while female employees were entitled to an early pension, in the same circumstances, at the age of 50. A contracted-out scheme operates as a replacement for the State Earnings Related Pension Scheme (SERPS). B challenged the legality of this.

Held Benefits paid by an employer in connection with redundancy were 'pay' within Article 141 EC (ex 119). Private occupational pensions were also 'pay', so the fact that pensions formed part of a statutory scheme or were contracted out to private insurance companies was irrelevant. No distinction could be drawn between contributory and non-contributory pensions for the purposes of Article 119. Thus, Article 119 prohibited the discrimination which B had encountered. The ECJ said:

Although it is true that many advantages granted by an employer also reflect considerations of social policy, the fact that a benefit is in the nature of pay cannot be called into question where the worker is entitled to receive the benefit in question from his employer by reason of the existence of the employment relationship.

The Court also established the principle that it is not enough that the overall package of remuneration received by men and women be equal: each element of the consideration paid to both sexes must be equal. The system of pay must be 'transparent', so that clear comparisons between men and women may be made.

The ECJ recognised that their judgment could have serious consequences for contracted-out pension schemes, especially as Member States could reasonably consider that Article 141 EC (ex 119) did not apply to payments under such schemes. All contributions paid into such schemes and the rate of payment calculations were based on different retirement ages for men and women. Hence, exceptionally, the ruling was made non-retroactive. Only workers who had made claims prior to the date of judgment (17 May 1990) were allowed to claim pension entitlements under *Barber*. (See Chapter 9 for further discussion.)

15.2.5 Survivors' benefits are included in Article 141 EC (ex 119)

Ten Oever v Stichting Case C-109/91

Held Barber v Guardian Royal Exchange Assurance Group was extended to cover survivors' benefits payable under occupational pension schemes. The fact that the benefit was not paid to the employee was irrelevant. The right is vested in the survivor by reason of the employment relationship between the employer and the survivor.

15.2.6 Transfer values and lump-sum options under occupational pension schemes are included in Article 141 EC (ex 119)

Neath v Hugh Steeper Ltd Case C-152/91

N was made redundant from HS at the age of 54. He claimed that his employer's contracted-out pension scheme was discriminatory in that he could not claim a full pension until 65 while female employees were entitled to do so at 60. He was refused an immediate pension, because this required the consent of his employers, but was entitled to either have his acquired pension rights transferred to another pension scheme, or have his pension deferred until his normal retirement age, that is, 65. At that time, he could ask for some of it to be converted into a capital sum. If he opted to have his pension transferred, he claimed that his transfer value would be lower than that of his female counterparts. If he kept his deferred pension and then claimed part of it as a lump sum, he would again receive less than female workers would. The Leeds industrial tribunal referred the matter to the ECJ.

Held Barber v Guardian Royal Exchange Assurance Group could be extended beyond pension benefits, to cover both transfer values and lump sum options under occupational pension schemes.

15.2.7 Right to join an occupational pension scheme within Article 141 EC (ex 119)

Vroege Case C-57/93

Held The restriction against retroactive effect introduced in *Barber v Guardian Royal Exchange Assurance Group* concerned only those kinds of discrimination which employers' pension schemes could 'reasonably have considered to be permissible'. It did *not* apply to discrimination in relation to membership of pension schemes. This had been held to be unlawful in *Bilka-Kaufhaus v Weber von Hartz* Case 170/84, decided on 13 May 1986, in a judgment which was not restricted in temporal terms. Thus, Article 141 EC (ex 119) could be relied upon, retroactively, to claim equal treatment in relation to *the right to join an occupational pension scheme* as from 8 April 1976, the date of the judgment in *Defrenne v SABENA (No 2)* Case 43/75, where Article 141 EC (ex 119) had first been given direct effect, but not before, as that judgment had also been made non-retroactive.

15.2.8 Compensation for unfair dismissal

R v Secretary of State for Employment ex p Seymour Smith and Perez Case 167/97

Seymour Smith and Perez were dismissed from their jobs after working for between one and two years. They were unable to bring unfair dismissal proceedings before the Industrial Tribunal because they had not worked continuously for the two year period required by the Unfair Dismissal (Variation of Qualifying Period) Order 1985. They argued that this was contrary to Article 5 of Directive 76/207/EEC in that it *prima facie* discriminated against women, in that a smaller proportion of women than men qualified under the 1985 order. In addition, the women argued that the right to compensation in unfair dismissal cases constituted 'pay' within the meaning of Article 141 EC (ex 199). The Court of Appeal held that the qualifying period of two years was discriminatory, but did not quash the order. The Secretary of State appealed to the House of Lords who sought a preliminary ruling from the ECJ.

The ECJ held that a judicial award of compensation for breach of a right not to be unfairly dismissed constitutes pay within the meaning of Article 141 (ex 119). The fact that certain benefits are paid after termination of the employment relationship does not prevent them from being within the nature of pay. Compensation for unfair dismissal is a form of deferred payment which the employee is entitled to by reason of his or her employment, but which is paid on termination of the employment relationship.

15.3   Equal work

Pickstone v Freemans plc (1989)

P and four other female warehouse operatives employed by Freemans complained of discrimination based purely on sex. They were paid the same as a male warehouse operative, but claimed that their work was of equal value to that done by a male warehouse checker, who was paid £4.22 more a week than they were. They argued that s 1(2)(c) of the Equal Pay Act 1970 applied. This allowed claims for equal pay for work of equal value. Freemans responded, first, that the women were employed on 'like work' for the same pay as male warehouse operatives, within s 1(2)(a) and, secondly, that a claim under s 1(2)(c) could only be made if their work was 'not ... work in relation to which [s 1(2)(a) or (b)] applies', therefore, they were not entitled to claim under s 1(2)(c).

The industrial tribunal rejected their claim, and this decision was upheld by the EAT. The Court of Appeal held that a claim under s 1(2)(c) was not possible, but a claim under Article 141 EC (ex 119) was possible.

Held The House of Lords rejected Freemans' appeal. Section 1(2)(c) of the Equal Pay Act 1970 was added by the Equal Pay (Amendment) Regulations 1983, which were passed in order to implement Directive 75/117/EEC (the Equal Pay Directive). The Lords were, therefore, prepared to give a purposive interpretation to this section. Lord Oliver said it was:

A construction which permits the section to operate as a proper fulfilment of the UK's obligations under the Treaty ...

Accordingly, a woman was only debarred from claiming equal pay under s 1(2)(c) if paras (a) or (b) applied *to the man with whom she claimed equality*. If the woman was employed on work of equal value to a man doing *another job* for the same employer, then she was entitled, under s 1(2)(c), to claim equal pay *with that man*, notwithstanding that there was another man doing the same work as her for equal pay. Thus, P and the other women were not debarred from claiming equal pay with male checkers, notwithstanding that there was a male warehouse operative who was paid the same as they were.

15.3.1 Directive 75/117/EEC – work to which equal value is attributed

Discrepancy in pay possible if objectively justified

Rummler v Dato-Druck GmbH Case 237/85

R was a packer placed at Group III on a wage scale by her employers, Dato-Druck GmbH, and not, as she thought she should be, at Group IV. She challenged the criteria on which this decision was based, alleging breach of Directive 75/117/EEC. Article 1 provides:

> The principle of equal pay for men and women outlined in Article 119[now 141] of the Treaty, hereinafter called 'principle of equal pay', means for the same work or for work to which equal value is attributed, the elimination of all discrimination on grounds of sex with regard to all aspects and conditions of remuneration.

> In particular, where a job classification system is used for determining pay, it must be based on the same criteria both men and women and so drawn up as to exclude any discrimination on grounds of sex.

The criteria included: muscular effort, fatigue and physical hardship. Her job involved lifting parcels weighing 20 kilos or more, which, she claimed, represented considerable physical work for a woman.

Held The criteria were not in breach of Article 1 of Directive 75/117/EEC as long as: (1) the system as a whole precluded discrimination on grounds of sex; and (2) the criteria employed were *objectively justified*. To be objectively justified they had to (a) be appropriate to the tasks to be carried out; and (b) correspond to a genuine need of the undertaking. Furthermore, the classification scheme as a whole had to take into account criteria for which each sex has a particular aptitude. Criteria which were based exclusively on the values of one sex ran a 'risk of discrimination'.

Handels og Kontorfunktionaerernes Forbundi Danmark v Dansk Arbejdsgiverførening for Danfoss Case 109/88

The Danish Employees' Union had given its support to a challenge brought by a group of women workers to criteria agreed by the Danish Employers' Association and utilised in employment contracts by many Danish firms, including Danfoss. Although basic pay was the same for men and women, salaries could be supplemented by the application of various, apparently neutral, criteria, including professional training, 'flexibility' and 'seniority'. As a result the average pay for female workers was 7% lower then that for male employees.

Held Where the application of neutral criteria was shown to result in systematic discrimination against female workers, this could only be because the employer applied it in an abusive manner. Where the average pay of females is lower than that of males, there is an onus of proof on the employer to justify the criteria. This was especially the case where there was a 'total lack of transparency' in the application of the criteria, that is, where it was not clear to those affected how the criteria were being used. Specifically, the criterion of 'flexibility' required justification in view of the greater difficulties faced by women in organising their time in a flexible manner. However, the criterion of 'seniority' was sufficiently transparent not to require justification.

Enderby v Frenchay Health Authority Case C-127/92

E, a speech therapist, was employed by the health authority on £10,106 pa. She claimed equality of pay with two males, also employed by the health authority – a clinical psychologist on £12,527 and a pharmacist on £14,106. These rates were required to be paid by employers under collective bargaining agreements within the NHS and approved by the Secretary of State. Her claim was rejected by the industrial tribunal and Employment Appeal Tribunal on the basis that the pay structures were specific to each profession.

On appeal, the Court of Appeal referred the matter to the ECJ, asking first whether the fact the differences in pay had been decided by collective bargaining processes meant there was no discrimination, and, secondly, whether the difference could be justified on other grounds.

Held The fact the differences in pay had been decided by collective bargaining processes was not sufficient justification. However, the Court accepted, in principle, an argument that certain employees were paid more to attract suitably qualified candidates. Thus the health authority could *try* to justify paying between £2,400 and £4,000 more to (predominantly male) clinical psychologists and pharmacists, than to (predominantly female) speech therapists. (The work was found to be of equal value.) Whether they could in fact do so would depend on the application of the necessity test by the national court.

15.4   Discrimination

15.4.1   Indirect discrimination – discrepancies in pay may be objectively justified

Jenkins v Kingsgate (Clothing Productions) Ltd Case 96/80

J was a female part time employee. All part time workers (all but one of whom was female) were paid 10% less than full time workers. The one part time male employee had actually retired but had been allowed to carry on working. J complained, and the Employment Appeal Tribunal referred the question to the ECJ. The Court refused to hold that there was necessarily discrimination, and introduced the objective justification principle:

> [T]he fact that work paid at time rates is remunerated at an hourly rate which varies according to the number of hours worked per week does not offend against the principle of equal pay laid down in Article 119 [now 141 EC] in so far as the difference in pay between part time and full time work is attributable to factors which are *objectively justified* and are *in no way related to any discrimination based on sex.*

One such factor, the Court considered, would be where the employer was seeking, for economic reasons, 'to encourage full time work irrespective of the sex of the worker'. However:

> ... if it is established that a considerably smaller percentage of women than of men perform the minimum number of weekly working hours required in order to be able to claim the full time hourly rate of pay, the inequality of pay will be contrary to Article 119 [now 141 EC] ... where, regard being had to the difficulties encountered by women in arranging to work that minimum number of hours per week, the pay policy of the undertaking in question cannot be explained by factors other than discrimination based on sex.

15.4.2 Differences in treatment are not always unlawful discrimination

Bird's Eye Walls v Roberts Case C-132/92

A bridging pension, designed to bridge the gap between the occupational pension scheme and the State pension they would receive on reaching retirement age, was paid *ex gratia* to employees of Bird's Eye compelled, on grounds of ill health, to take early retirement. R challenged this.

Held This was not discriminatory even though women received less than men. The mechanisms used for calculating the bridging pension were gender neutral; R's lower pension reflected her lower contribution rate, for which she had freely opted.

15.5 Article 141 EC (ex 119) not limited to contemporaneous employment

Macarthys Ltd v Smith Case 129/79

S was employed by Macarthys as a warehouse manageress. She was being paid less than her male predecessor (£50 compared to £60 a week). The male employee had left the post some four months previously. She challenged the discrepancy, but a majority of the Court of Appeal thought that s 1(2) of the Employment Protection Act 1975 limited the right of equal pay to men and women engaged in like work to *contemporaneous employment*, because it refers to 'where the woman is employed', and not *sequential employment*. However, the matter was referred to the ECJ for guidance.

Held The application of Article 141 EC (ex 119) is not necessarily limited to men and women engaged in contemporaneous employment for the same employer. However, a difference in pay between two workers occupying the same post at different times might be explained by other factors, unconnected with a difference in sex. This question would be for the national court or tribunal to decide as a matter of fact.

15.6 Directive 76/207/EEC – equal treatment in the context of employment

15.6.1 Scope of the Equal Treatment Directive – Article 1: access to employment

Jackson and Cresswell v Chief Adjudication Officer Cases C-63 and 64/91
Two single mothers, one engaged in vocational training, the other in part time work, claimed entitlement to supplementary benefit and income support, respectively. They were refused, and claimed this contravened Directive 76/207/EEC.

Held The benefits did not fall within the Directive. Article 1 provides:

The purpose of this Directive is to put into effect in the Member States the principle of equal treatment for men and women as regards access to employment, including promotion, and to vocational training and as regards working conditions ...

Although the benefits might discriminate against the single parent, the majority of whom were women, they did not relate to access to employment, including access to employment via vocational training.

Meyers v Adjudication Officer Case C-116/94
M, the single mother of a three year old child, applied for family credit, a benefit payable under the Social Security Act 1986 to supplement low paid workers who were also responsible for a child. She was refused because her income was above the statutory minimum. She then argued that this constituted indirect discrimination against single parents, the majority of whom were women. If she had been in a couple, her husband or partner would have been able to help to look after her child while she was at work. However, because she was single, she had to pay for child care. If this payment was deducted from her income, she would be eligible for family credit.

Held Family credit was within Directive 76/207/EEC. The Court rejected the UK's objection that the benefit did not cover 'access to' employment because it was payable to those already in employment. It dealt with 'access to' employment because *it encouraged people to take low paid jobs*. The fact that a benefit formed part of a social security system did not necessarily take it outside of Directive (76/207/EEC). Family credit had a dual benefit – keeping low paid workers in employment, as well as helping them meet family expenses. Family credit was within the Directive even though the benefit, if paid to a couple, was automatically paid to the woman, even if she was not working; and was payable for 26 weeks, even if the circumstances changed.

The ECJ also rejected the argument by the UK that family credit did not come within 'working conditions', because the Directive only concerned conditions in the contract of employment. The scope of the directive could not be limited to what was provided in the contract. Instead, the Court stated that 'working conditions' referred to the whole 'employment relationship'.

15.6.2 Scope of the Equal Treatment Directive – Article 5: conditions governing dismissal – discriminatory retirement ages

Burton v British Railways Board Case 19/81

B, aged 58, challenged British Rail's voluntary redundancy scheme, under which men were entitled to apply for redundancy at 60 while women could at 55. He would have had no success with a challenge based on the Sex Discrimination Act 1975, because of s 6(4), which (prior to amendment by the Sex Discrimination Act 1986 making discriminatory retirement ages illegal) excluded, from the scope of the Act, 'provisions' in relation to death or retirement. B sought to rely on Directive 76/207/EEC.

Held In principle, Article 5(1) of the Directive applied. Article 5(1) provides:

> Application of the principle of equal treatment with regard to working conditions, including the conditions governing dismissal, means that men and women shall be guaranteed the same conditions without discrimination on grounds of sex.

The word 'dismissal' was wide enough to cover even a voluntary termination of the relationship of employment. However, because the scheme's retirement ages were calculated by reference to, and were tied to, the State retirement ages, Article 7 of Directive 79/7/EEC was also to be applied. This allows Member States to exclude form the scope of the equal treatment principle 'the determination of pensionable age for the purposes of granting old age and retirement pensions and the possible consequences thereof for other benefits'. Thus, B's claim failed.

Marshall v Southampton and South West Hampshire Area Health Authority (Teaching) Case 152/84

M, who was employed by the area health authority as a senior dietician, was seeking to challenge its compulsory retirement age of 60 for women, compared with 65 for men. In 1980, she had been forced to retire, aged 62, despite expressing her willingness to continue until aged 65. She brought an action for unfair dismissal, contrary to the Sex Discrimination Act 1975 and Article 5(1). The industrial tribunal dismissed the action based on the Sex Discrimination Act, because of s 6(4), but upheld the claim based on Article 5(1) of the Directive. The Employment Appeal Tribunal agreed there was no action based on the Sex Discrimination Act, and reversed the decision on Article 5(1), which, it said, did not have direct effect between M and the area health authority. The Court of Appeal referred to the ECJ.

Held Following *Burton v British Railways Board* Case 19/81, the retirement scheme was a 'condition governing dismissal' within Article 5. However, distinguishing *Burton*, Article 7 only allows the State to exclude from the equal treatment principle 'the determination of pensionable age *for the purposes of granting old age and retirement pensions and the possible consequences thereof for other benefits'*. It does *not* exclude from the principle the determination of pensionable age for other purposes, such as *for retirement*, which was the case here. Thus, M's claim was allowed.

Roberts v Tate & Lyle Industries Ltd Case 151/84

R, aged 53, was made redundant from Tate & Lyle's Liverpool depot. Tate & Lyle's occupational pension scheme offered immediate accelerated pension rights to all employees made redundant if aged 55 or over. (This replaced a previous arrangement whereby immediate pensions were payable to women aged 55, but not to men until aged 60.) R was therefore not entitled to an immediate pension. She claimed Tate & Lyle's new scheme was discriminatory, since women were not entitled to it until five years before the State retirement age (60), whereas men were entitled to it 10 years before that age (65). A 10 year rule for men and women would have brought Mrs Roberts within the ambit of an immediate pension.

Held Following *Marshall*, Tate & Lyle's compulsory early retirement scheme was within Article 5 of Directive 76/207/EEC, as a condition governing dismissal, and so the equal treatment principle applied. The exemption in Directive 79/7/EEC again did not apply, for the same reason – the scheme referred to retirement ages, not pensionable ages. However, R's claim still failed. The early retirement scheme applied at age 55 for both men and women, therefore it was not discriminatory.

15.6.3 Conditions governing unfair dismissal

R v Secretary of State for Employment ex p Seymour Smith and Perez Case 167/97
For facts, see above, 15.2.8.

The ECJ was also asked whether the qualifying period of two years for claimants to bring unfair dismissal proceedings was contrary to Directive 76/207/EEC.

Held The ECJ held that it is for the national court, taking into account all the material legal and factual circumstances, to determine the point in time in which the legality of a rule is to be assessed. The national court, in making the assessment, must take into account available statistics to see whether a considerably smaller percentage of women than men are able to fulfil the requirement imposed by the rule. If that is the case, there is indirect discrimination, unless the rule is justified by objective factors unrelated to any discrimination based on sex.

15.7 Discrimination following 'gender reassignment'

P v S and Cornwall County Council Case C-13/94
In 1991, P was engaged as a manager in a college operated by Cornwall County Council. In April 1992, he informed S, the director of studies in the college, that he intended to undergo 'gender reassignment', comprising a period of dressing and behaving as a women, to be followed by surgery to provide the physical attributes of a woman. By September 1992, he had undergone minor operations. He was then dismissed. He claimed this was unlawful sexual discrimination.

Truro industrial tribunal found that the reason for his dismissal was his decision to undergo gender reassignment, but that, under English law, he was still a man. The Sex Discrimination Act 1975 did not apply because that only caught situations in which a man or woman was treated differently because they belonged to one or other of the sexes. This was not the case here – P would have been dismissed had he been a woman prior to undergoing gender reassignment. The question was whether EC law applied.

Held Article 5(1) of Directive 76/207 prevented the dismissal of a transsexual for a reason related to gender reassignment. The Court rejected the UK's submission that the dismissal was not discriminatory on the ground that the employer would still have dismissed P had he been a woman who had undergone treatment in order to become a man. The right not to be discriminated against on the grounds of sex was one of the fundamental human rights whose observance the Court had a duty to ensure. Accordingly, the scope of the Directive could not be confined simply to discrimination based on the fact that a person was of one or other sex. It also applied to discrimination arising, as in the present case, from gender reassignment. Such discrimination was based, essentially, if not exclusively, on the sex of the person. A transsexual dismissed because they intended to undergo, or had undergone, gender reassignment, was being treated unfavourably by comparison with persons of the sex to which he or she was deemed to belong prior to the reassignment.

15.8 Discrimination relating to sexual orientation

R v Secretary of State for Defence ex p Smith (1996)

Four servicemen challenged, by way of judicial review, the decision to discharge them from the armed forces on the sole ground that they were homosexual. They argued that the grounds for discharge were irrational, contrary to Article 8 of the European Convention of Human Rights and in breach of Article 2 of the Equal Treatment Directive.

Held Simon Brown LJ in the Court of Appeal held that the Equal Treatment Directive did not apply to discrimination on the grounds of sexual orientation.

Grant v South West Trains Ltd Case C-249/96

Under the terms of BRT employment contracts, certain travel concessions could be granted to a worker's 'spouse and dependants' or for one 'common law opposite sex partner', the latter being subject to a statutory declaration that a meaningful relationship had existed for two or more years. Ms Grant, who was an employee of SWT, applied for a travel concession for her lesbian partner. This was refused and Ms Grant commenced proceedings in the industrial tribunal, arguing that the refusal was in breach of the Equal Pay Act 1970, Article 141 EC (ex 119) of the Treaty and/or Directive 76/207/EEC. The matter was referred to the ECJ.

Held The ECJ held:

- concessionary travel fell within the ambit of Article 141 EC (ex 119), not Directive 76/207/EEC;
- the SWT rules applied regardless of the sex of the worker concerned and therefore did not constitute discrimination based on sex;
- Community law as it stood (see note, below), however, did not regard homosexual relationships as equivalent to marriage or stable relationships outside marriage between persons of the opposite sex; the position could only be changed by legislation;
- the ECJ said that the decision in *P v S* (see above, 15.7) was limited to gender reassignment and did not apply to differences in treatment based upon a persons sexual orientation.

Note
The Treaty of Amsterdam makes specific provision in Article 6A to take appropriate legislative action to combat discrimination based on sexual orientation.

15.9 Directive 76/207/EEC does not have horizontal direct effect

Duke v GEC Reliance Ltd (1988)

D had been forced to retire at 60. She argued that this was contrary to ss 1(1)(a) and s 6(2)(b) of the Sex Discrimination Act 1975. Section 1(1)(a) provides:

> A person discriminates against a woman in any circumstances relevant for the purposes of any provision of this Act if (a) on the ground of her sex he treats her less favourably than he treats or would treat a man.

GEC responded that, according to s 6(4) of the Act, s 6(2) did not apply to 'provision in relation to ... retirement'. The industrial tribunal dismissed her claim, and that decision was upheld by the employment appeal tribunal and the Court of Appeal. She appealed to the House of Lords, arguing that EC law required the 1975 Act to be construed so as to give effect to the Directive 76/207/EEC (the Equal Treatment Directive).

Held The 1975 Act had been amended by the Sex Discrimination Act 1986, which implemented the Equal Treatment Directive. The amendment was *not*, however, made retrospective. Duke's imposed retirement had occurred prior to the coming into force of the 1986 Act. Lord Templeman refused to construe the 1975 Act as requested. The 1975 Act was not implementing legislation and could not be interpreted as requested. The 1986 Act was implementing legislation, but didn't apply to events prior to its enactment. Lord Templeman was reluctant to give horizontal direct effect to a Directive, by the back door:

> It would be most unfair [to GEC] to distort the construction of the 1975 Act in order to accommodate the Equal Treatment Directive ... As between [Duke] and [GEC], the Equal Treatment Directive did not have direct effect and [GEC] could not reasonably be expected to reduce to precision the opaque language ...

15.10 Derogation from the equal treatment principle – Article 2(2) and (3)

Johnston v Chief Constable of the Royal Ulster Constabulary Case 222/84

J had been an unarmed member of the RUC Reserve for some years. The Chief Constable had adopted various policies concerning women's roles within the RUC. These included not equipping women with firearms, nor training them in the use of firearms, nor asking women to perform general duties (which might involve the use of firearms). Female officers would be performing certain roles allocated to women only. J had been performing general duties, and when her contract came up for renewal in 1980, the Chief Constable refused to renew it, applying the new policy. She brought an action against the RUC alleging discrimination.

J was unable to rely on UK legislation, because Article 53 of the Sex Discrimination (Northern Ireland) Order 1976 exempted action taken 'for the purpose of safeguarding national security or of protecting public safety or public order'. Instead, she relied on Directive 76/207/EEC. The Chief Constable responded that to allow women to carry arms would increase the risk of their becoming targets for assassination and the danger of their firearms falling into the wrong hands. It was further argued that an analogy should be drawn with Article 39(3) EC (ex 48(3)) of the EC Treaty, allowing derogations from non-discrimination provisions of EC law in the interests of public policy and public security.

Held The ECJ, while stating that the derogation should be applied strictly, upheld the RUC's change of policy. While a derogation could not be applied to activities *per se*, it was permissible to take into account the context in which specific activities took place. Here, the sensitive situation of Northern Ireland meant that the derogation in Article 2(2) was met. Article 2(2) allows for derogation from the equal treatment principle for 'occupational activities … for which … the sex of the worker constitutes a determining factor'. However, where such derogation was allowed, the situation must be reviewed periodically, in order to ensure that the justification for it still existed. The Court also stressed that the derogation was subject to the principle of proportionality, which was a question for the national courts to decide.

Held The ECJ also held that the RUC's policy was not justifiable under Article 2(3). This provides that a derogation from the principle of equal treatment is provided for 'provisions concerning the protection of women, particularly as regards pregnancy and maternity'. That provision is designed to protect women's *biological condition*.

Hofmann v Barmer Ersatzkasse Case 184/83

A father claimed six months' leave following the birth of his child while the mother went to work. He argued that German law, which granted maternity but not paternity leave, was discriminatory.

Held Article 2(3) protected two types of female need: (1) the biological condition of women during and after pregnancy; and (2) the relationship between mother and child during the period following birth. It was *not* designed to cover the organisation of a family, or the division of responsibility between parents.

15.11 Positive discrimination – Article 2(4)

Kalanke v Freie Hansestadt Bremen Case C-450/93

K was a male candidate shortlisted along with G for a post in the Bremen Parks Department, where they were both already employed. Both were equally qualified, but the Bremen law on Equal Treatment for Men and Women in the Public Service 1990 provided that women who had the same qualifications as men applying for promotion to the same post were to be given priority if women were under-represented (that is, comprising less than half the staff in the relevant personnel group). K was recommended for promotion, but his application was rejected on the basis of the 1990 law. The Federal Labour Court referred the question whether the German law was compatible with Article 2(1) and (4) of Directive 76/207/EEC. The latter allows Member States to introduce 'measures to promote equal opportunities for men and women, in particular by removing existing inequalities which affect women's opportunities'.

Held National laws which guaranteed women absolute and unconditional priority for appointment or promotion went beyond 'promoting' equal opportunities and overstepped the exception allowed in Article 2(4). The German law was discriminatory and precluded by Article 2(1).

Marschall v Land Nordrhein Westfalen Case C-409/95

A German regional law stated that, where there were fewer women than men in certain high grade career jobs, women were to be given priority treatment for promotion in circumstances where the candidates were of equal suitability and competence. However, the law contained an exception (referred to by the ECJ as a 'saving clause') that, where there were specific circumstances relating to the male applicant, the balance could be tilted in favour of him. The German authorities argued that this rather imprecise approach allowed for a greater degree of flexibility than a quota system.

Held The ECJ held that, whilst a rule which guaranteed 'absolute and unconditional priority' to women was unlawful, a rule such as the one in this case, which contains a 'saving clause', would be lawful where the rule counteracts the prejudicial effects on female candidates of stereotyped attitudes concerning the role and capacities of women. Thus, the German regional law was lawful and within Article 2(4) because it guaranteed that male candidates would be subject to an objective assessment which took account of all criteria specific to the individual candidates and would override the priority given to the female candidates where one or more of those criteria tilted the balance in favour of the male candidate.

15.12 Protection for pregnant women under the Equal Treatment Directive

Dekker v Stichting Vormingscentrum voor Jong Volwassenen (VJV Centrum) Plus Case C-177/88

An employer withdrew a job offer made to D when he discovered she was pregnant. He argued he could not afford to employ a replacement as well.

Held Refusing to employ a woman because she was pregnant was direct discrimination and could not be justified because of financial difficulties.

Webb v EMO Air Cargo (UK) Ltd Case C-32/93

W had been engaged to replace another employee who had become pregnant. Two weeks later she discovered she was herself pregnant. She was promptly dismissed. Glidewell LJ in the Court of Appeal concluded that dismissal on grounds of pregnancy might *sometimes* amount to direct discrimination. On the facts, however, where W had been employed specifically to provide pregnancy cover, there was no discrimination. He thought that, if a male employee was employed just to cover for a male worker requiring a hip replacement operation and then discovered he also needed an operation, the employer would be entitled to dismiss him. There was no difference between that situation and W's. W appealed to the Lords, from where a reference to the ECJ was made.

Held Following *Dekker v Stichting Vormingscentrum voor Jong Volwassenen*, the dismissal was illegal. It was incorrect, as the Court of Appeal had done, to compare the situation of a woman who became pregnant, with that of a man with a medical and even more so with a non-medical condition.

Brown v Rentokil Ltd Case C-394/96

In August 1990, Brown informed her employers that she was pregnant. She then became ill as a result of her pregnancy and was unable to work from mid-August. Under her contract of employment, she could be dismissed if continuously absent from work due to illness for more than 26 weeks. Brown did not have the two years' continuous employment required for receipt of statutory maternity pay, which allowed an employee to absent herself from work from the beginning of the 11th week before the expected date of the birth. Brown was dismissed and she commenced proceedings before the Industrial Tribunal. The case was appealed to the House of Lords, who sought a preliminary ruling from the ECJ on whether Articles 2(1) and 5(1) of Directive 76/207/EEC precluded the dismissal of a female employee at any time during her pregnancy as a result of absence through illness arising from that pregnancy.

Held The ECJ held that dismissal of a pregnant worker for absences due to incapacity for work resulting from her pregnancy was linked to the inherent risk of pregnancy and, therefore, had to be based essentially on the fact of the pregnancy. Such a dismissal would be discriminatory and would render the provisions of Directive 76/207/EEC ineffective.

15.13 Compensation for breach of the equal treatment principles – Article 6

Marshall v Southampton and South West Hampshire Area Health Authority (Teaching) (No 2) Case C-271/91

In *Marshall v Southampton and South West Hampshire Area Health Authority (Teaching)* Case 152/84, the ECJ had upheld M's complaint of discrimination. In the second case, the sole question was the amount of compensation to which M was entitled from her erstwhile employers. The industrial tribunal in Southampton, mindful of its duty to provide a 'real and effective' remedy, awarded her £19,405 compensation. The award included £7,710 by way of interest. This was more than she was entitled to under then British law, s 65(2) of the Sex Discrimination Act 1975, because that Act had specified a maximum award of £6,250 and with no provision for interest. The tribunal, however, held that s 65(2) was in breach of Article 6. This provides:

> Member States shall introduce into their national legal systems such measures as are necessary to enable all persons who consider themselves wronged by failure to apply to them the principle of equal treatment … to pursue their claims by judicial process after possible recourse to other competent authorities.

The authority appealed, and the employment appeal tribunal cut her award on the ground that Article 6 did not have direct effect. M then appealed to the Court of Appeal, without success, and again, to the House of Lords, who referred the question to the ECJ.

Held Each case should be judged on its own circumstances. Where, however, a Member State has adopted financial compensation as the remedy available in the event of breach of Article 6, then such compensation had to make good any loss or damage sustained, albeit within the applicable national rules. However, s 65(2) was in breach of Article 6 because it set an upper limit and did not take into account inflation. The House of Lords duly set aside the decisions of the Employment Appeal Tribunal and Court of Appeal, restoring the decision of the industrial tribunal in *Southampton*.

15.11.1 Compensation measured under tortious principles

Ministry of Defence v Cannock (1995)

Several women, including C and H, were dismissed from the UK's armed services, because they became pregnant, between 1980 and 1989. Following *Marshall v Southampton and South West Hampshire Area Health Authority (Teaching) (No 2)*, they brought compensation claims, which were allowed by industrial tribunals in the UK. The Ministry of Defence appealed.

Held The Employment Appeal Tribunal, allowing a series of claims for compensation, held that the correct measure of damages in cases of sex discrimination brought under the Directive was *tortious* rather than *contractual*. The women should, therefore, be awarded damages to place them in the position they would have been in had they not been dismissed. Some of the awards were substantial. C was awarded £173,000; H £156,000 plus interest of £18,000.

Index